Dragons of Thin Air

A Most Unusual
Fear of Flying Course

Dragons of Thin Air

A Most Unusual Fear of Flying Course

Doug Worrall

FIRST EDITION

Text by Doug Worrall
Illustrations by Doug and Kerri Worrall

ISBN: 978-1450549561
ISBN-10: 145054956X

All entities appearing in this work are fictitious.
Any resemblance to real entities, living, dead, actual or historical,
is purely coincidental. And, in case you were wondering,
no dragons or humans were harmed in the making
of this book.

Dedication

This book is dedicated, with love,
to Kerri, Angus and Kiara.

Acknowledgements

This book would not exist without the generous input of time and knowledge from aviation psychology and Fear of Flying specialist Rod Jepsen (PortPsych, Melbourne Australia). Thanks, Rod.

Also thankyou to the members of PAN, the Peer Assistance Network providing confidential care to Australian pilots and their families, for your support, feedback and editorial input.

DRAGONS OF THIN AIR:
A MOST UNUSUAL FEAR OF FLYING COURSE

---- *PART THREE: COME FLY WITH ME* ----

Introductions

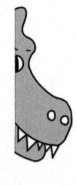

Walk the Walk!

The Walker family had spent too many vacations at home because of fear of flying. While their friends explored other countries and their relatives hoopla'd in far-off cities, the Walkers stayed at home. Again.

Their fears were not the same; after all, what two people are alike? Larry was afraid of crashing; Louise was afraid of panicking and making a fool of herself; Their daughter Jane thought that terrorists wanted to eat her. Only the youngest, Johnny, was not afraid. Being part of this family, however, meant that it was only a matter of time before he, too, developed fear.

They may not have travelled far, or often, but they knew their home town well. That's why they were surprised, while walking the streets one day, to see a towering building where one had not been the day before. Reaching for the clouds, this magnificent building demanded investigation.

Around the entrance were several advertisements for a *Fear of Flying* course. This caused some discussion amongst the family for, while the three oldest were all afraid to fly, none wanted to admit it. Each found it easy to avoid flying by blaming other family members.

Johnny saw an opportunity to niggle his older sister. "That course would suit you, you big yellow chicken. Chickens don't fly!"

Jane scowled and poked her brother just a little harder than was necessary. "The last time *you* went on a plane you cried like a baby." She knew that he'd cried because his ears hurt, not because he was afraid, but she still used it.

Larry could see that this discussion was going no place good, so he intervened. "Kids, a bit of quiet please. You can't help being yellow."

Johnny gave a gappy grin, enjoying Dad's sense of humour, and Jane punched her father affectionately in the stomach — perhaps just a little too hard.

"Dad! You and Mum are just as freaked about flying as I am. Why don't we do something about it?"

The wind knocked out of him by his daughter's punch, Larry could not explain that he and Louise couldn't afford a *Fear of Flying* course. He also couldn't give any of the other usual excuses — *we don't have the time; I've never heard of this company; this building shouldn't even exist.* Instead, gasping, he simply scowled at his daughter.

Looking out from inside the lobby I could see that the Walkers were ready; I opened the door wide and smiled my toothy welcome.

"Come in, come in. You are just in time!"

They seemed surprised, and perhaps a little shocked.

"You gotta be kidding!" exclaimed Larry, an eyebrow raised.

"Oh my gosh!" gasped Louise, her hand over her mouth.

"Awesome!" blurted Jane, cooled out by my impressive stature.

They may have said some other things too.

The politest response came from the youngest; Johnny bravely walked to the door, looked me up and down, and spoke.

"Excuse me Sir. Are you, by any chance, a dragon?"

"Yes, of course," I replied matter-of-factly to what was a rather obvious question. No time for small talk, however.

"Come along. We are due to start!"

Humans have trembled at the thought of dragons for thousands of years. It must have made sense to the Walkers that I would know a thing or two about fear. Still, they did not leap at my invitation.

Larry, a troubled look on his face, thought he knew all about dragons. "Aren't dragons supposed to eat people?"

What an appalling suggestion! "No, good heavens, no!"

Still, I thought, glancing at my clawed feet, *there was a time...* It was obvious that Larry had heard these old stories so I added, under my breath, "Not any more."

Louise gave me the chilling look of disbelief that she usually saves for used-car salesmen. I shuddered.

I suppose I had to explain. "Look, that was a long time ago. What dragons really do now is to help humans understand fear."

My partial explanation did not help and, with the sad realisation of a second-rate salesman who has been told "I'll think about it and get back to you," I knew I was losing them.

I tried a different tack. "Look, my *Fear of Flying* course is like nothing you've ever seen. It has fun and games. It has puppies. It is about to start, so don't miss out!"

That was good enough for the kids; they both ran past me into the lobby. Unable to think of a good reason not to save their children, Larry and Louise followed them inside.

I smiled and closed the door. Humans are putty in my hands!

**FEAR OF FLYING
COURSE**

<u>**STUDENT FEEDBACK**</u>

Name: Louise Walker

Question 1: What Did You Think of the Facilities?

From the impressive exterior of the building and the polished marble in the lobby I had expected a very professional presentation room.

I thought there would be tables, chairs and a water cooler; I thought there would be rows of chairs, carpet and a window.

Instead, your presentation room was a storeroom in the basement.

OK, the shelves and junk had been pushed to one side and four chairs had been lined up facing the wall. You even had a whiteboard.

But call it a "presentation room?"

Between the stink and the dim light, I'd only call it a presentation room if I'd been living under the kitchen sink for my entire life.

I also thought it was strange that there were exactly four chairs. It was as if you knew we were coming.

The Short Fear of Flying Course

As I showed the Walkers down to my fabulous Multimedia Presentation Room I could tell that they were impressed. Their silence as they looked around betrayed their feelings of awe.

The book I had read about how to talk to humans explained that politeness and modesty are highly regarded, so I talked down the facilities.

"Please take a seat. I apologise for the size of our presentation room. This course is somewhat experimental and I do not yet have a large budget."

Oops! I shouldn't have said that!

"Experimental?" asked Larry with the look of someone who had just eaten earwax after being told it was jam. "What is your success rate?"

Oh well, I suppose they should know...

"Er, this is the first time I have run this course. You are my first customers."

Actually, this was kind of amusing. I chuckled, and told them why. "Afraid of flying, yet you are test pilots!"

"Crash test dummies, more like it!" harrumphed Louise, sitting down on the chair at the end. She stared vacantly at the wall where there should have been a window.

The rest of the family took their seats, and I began.

"Welcome to the inaugural Fear Dragons *Fear of Flying* Course. My name is Felix. I will be your instructor."

I started writing notes on the whiteboard. I'd spent weeks preparing the course and was confident that it included everything important about flying. As I wrote the entire text of the course up on the whiteboard I hoped that the Walkers would not grow impatient.

Actually, it did not take long.

When I had finished I stood back and looked at what I had written, checking that I had not made any mistakes. *Perfect!* I had included everything that they needed to know to cure their fear.

I told them, simply, "There. That's it."

Realising the perfection of my words I added, "Perhaps you should make some notes."

The kids, Johnny and Jane, giggled. Louise gaped and asked, "Flying is safe and fun? Is that it?"

Larry looked toward the door. He was right—it was time to go.

"Yes, yes. Well, I hope you enjoyed the course. Off you go. I've got to get this room turned back into a storeroom by this afternoon, so *bye-bye!* Thanks for coming."

Johnny leaned toward his father. "Dad, that is the lamest course I have ever seen. Dogs know more about flying than this guy."

"Shhh! I know it is lame. Perhaps we *should* leave."

Do these people think a dragon cannot hear whispering? I was outraged but I wasn't sure who had spoken.

"WHO IS TALKING???" I demanded.

Johnny quickly pointed at his father.

As calmly as I could, with steam rising from my nostrils, I stood in front of Larry. "If you have got something to say, Mister Whisperer, then share it with the rest of us!"

"Er," said Larry nervously, "Its just that your course seems a little... short. Surely there is more to it than that."

How dare he? My grandfather might have roasted this insolent creature and then eaten the charred remains.

Despite his rudeness, however, I realised that perhaps he had a point.

I grumbled, "You may be right Larry, although that is basically all there is to it. I could pad it out a bit I suppose."

The kids seemed pleased.

"Yay!" cheered Johnny.

"Give us a show!" cheered Jane.

The trouble was that I had put all of my best stuff into the words I had written on the whiteboard. *What else was there to tell them?*

I realised my task was not going to be as easy as I had thought. Sure, I'm a Fear Dragon... my day job is to cause fear, after all. Even your average Fear Dragon can terrify a human as easily as snapping his fingers, and I'm one of the best. Today, however, I needed to do the opposite—I needed to help these humans; I needed to ease their fears and show them that flying is safe.

That's when I remembered my own fear training all those years ago, and the wise words of Kaniza, himself a legend amongst the Fear Dragons: *"Felix, to make people afraid you need to know the truth, and then you must bend it and twist it, or avoid it like the plague."*

Kaniza had then shown me a slideshow about how safe flying really is and I remember thinking afterwards that convincing humans to be afraid of flying was going to be impossible. Of course, I got over it. In fact I went on to become a champion at creating fear, but I realised now that this was just the kind of stuff the Walkers needed to see.

I told the Walkers what I was thinking. "I do have some *Fear of Flying* slides around here somewhere, although I'm not really sure I should show them to you. They are... er... classified."

I growled with indecision. Should I? Dare I? *What can it hurt?*

"Oh, all right. Why not? Just give me a moment..."

It had been some years since I had seen those slides, but I was fairly sure they were somewhere in this storeroom. I grunted and grumbled as I searched one box then another. *Humans are so demanding and difficult! Always wanting to know more.*

Eventually, however, I found what I was looking for behind an old box of plastic rats. Returning to the front of the Multimedia Presentation Room, with a projector and a box of slides under my arm, I hummed a cheerful tune.

Johnny seemed unimpressed with the modern technology I was setting up. "How come you are not using a computer display system? And a Powerpoint presentation? Everyone uses that stuff these days."

"I prefer the old ways," I gruffly replied as I loaded the slides. *These humans really can be rude at times.*

Then we were ready, and expectation filled the room. Larry, Louise and Jane were as quiet as shivering mice fearful of being eaten by the town cat, and Johnny had a big smile on his face.

I pressed the slide advance button and so began my new, improved and expanded "Most Unusual Fear of Flying Course."

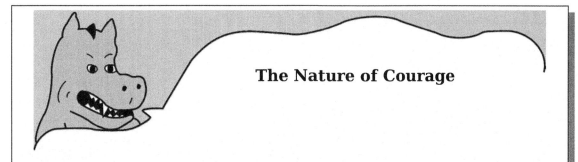

The Nature of Courage

Don't let anyone make you feel bad about being a nervous flyer. Even the bravest people are afraid of something... they often just don't tell anyone about it.

The most awesome displays of courage come from people dealing with their fears.

That is REAL courage, no matter what anyone says.

**Fear will try to keep you on the ground.
To allow this is YOUR choice!**

PART ONE

Fear

Felix's Most Unusual
FEAR OF FLYING COURSE
SLIDE PRESENTATION

Lesson 1: Some People Are Afraid to Fly

It makes sense that some people are afraid. The idea of sitting inside a tin can, high in the sky, can be challenging.

Here is an important thing to remember:

If you have a fear of flying <u>you are not alone</u>.

This saying has two meanings:

1. There are lots of other people who are afraid;
2. There are people who can help you with your fear.

What do I mean by lots? Nearly one third of all people experience some fear of flying. That's *millions* of people. *Fear of flying* is one of the most common fears in the modern world.

There *are* people who understand and can help you to deal with your fear. This course is one example. We will discuss some of the other assistance available later.

Life Before Fear

It can be hard to remember what it was like *before* anxiety and fear became a part of your life.

People do not start out with fear. A baby, for example, is not afraid of anything. *Fear of flying,* like all fears, **develops** over time. It can occur gradually, or it may begin with a single disturbing event.

Once upon a time you were calm and fearless. Our goal is to return you to that way of life.

Introducing an Amazing Storyteller...

I am going to introduce you to a truly amazing storyteller—an artist with the ability to create amazing worlds and fearsome creatures out of nothing but words and memories.

This storyteller creates fire-breathing dragons so frighteningly real, so alive, so awful that you will want to expel your breakfast in terror!

I am talking about a true genius of fiction. This genius is able to create a story that will stay with you—a story that will follow you into every waking moment and shape how you see the world and your place in it.

Who is the creative genius I am talking about?

It is **you!**

MASTER
STORYTELLER

You *are the creator of amazing tales!*

The Problem with Fear of Flying

If you suffer from *fear of flying* you will miss out on some of life's great adventures because you won't fly. Visits with family, work opportunities and exotic adventures all cause problems.

You might do **anything** to avoid getting on a plane.

Or, you might fly but hate every second. Time spent on a plane, at the airport or even just thinking about flying may be a special kind of torture best saved for criminals and politicians.

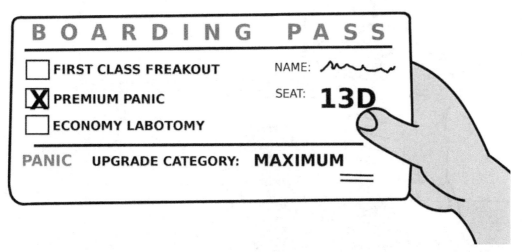

Love it or hate it, flying is a part of our modern world. Coming to terms with air travel is possible but it will take some courage.

I know you have it in you!

Psychology 101

I knew that boarding passes sometimes
trigger a nervous reaction from fearful flyers so I paused the slideshow
to see how my students were doing.

"Questions anyone? Anything troubling you so far?"

Louise politely raised her hand. *Fabulous!* Questions are an
opportunity for an instructor to demonstrate great knowledge and
reinforce a position of superiority over his students. I grinned widely
and waved her to speak.

"How does an overweight lizard know anything about *fear of flying?*"

Overweight? Why you scrawny... I growled and fumes rose from my nostrils. I'd cut back to four dogs a day. *How could I be overweight?*

Louise realised I was upset and quickly explained herself. "What I meant to say, Felix, is how can *you* help us? After all, we are nothing like you. And we all have different fears."

"I don't," said Johnny who was, so far, blissfully ignorant of fear, but certainly the other three had an assortment of issues.

"Well, you are kind of right and kind of wrong about having different fears. You have different *reasons* for fear, but fear itself is much the same for everybody. Would you like to hear some technical words that I learned from my psychologist?"

"No, not really," said Larry.

"Certainly not," said Louise.

"Nope," said Johnny.

"You have a psychologist?" asked Jane.

I smiled and, with a quiet nod, replied "Sure."

The older Walkers seemed surprised at this but Johnny gave an understanding nod and, for no good reason, added "*I* visited a cyclist once. She told me to get on my bike."

Jane groaned at her brother's misconception. Johnny had made the common mistake of confusing a "cyclist" with a "psychologist."

She explained to her brother, "Johnny, a cyclist balances on two wheels, but a psychologist can help you balance your mind. A psychologist helps you to understand how your brain works and gives you strategies for using it better."

She's a smart one!

"Very good Jane. Everyone is afraid of something. If fear is getting in the way of a full and happy life sometimes a psychologist can help."

Larry still didn't get it. "Yeah, but you're a dragon. How come dragons need psychologists?"

"People think that a big, tough dragon like me must not be afraid of anything, but it's not true. You'd be surprised at how many Fear

Dragons visit with Doc Leroy. It's perfectly normal, you know."

I told the Walkers about my psychologist, Doctor Leroy Amygdala. He is a great guy who listens to my problems and very rarely laughs at me. He says "Uh-huh" a lot while I'm talking and suggests things I can try to calm my mind.

For example, he had me try a deep breathing technique. We'll talk about some of those later. I have to say that I did not find it helpful, but most humans do.

Louise had heard about deep breathing and wanted to know why it hadn't worked for me. I explained, "Louise, when a dragon does deep breathing things get incinerated!"

I also warned the Walkers about the size of the words that some psychologists use. I knew they did not want to hear complicated technical words, so I told them anyway:

aerophobia = fear of flying

acrophobia = fear of heights

claustrophobia = fear of enclosed spaces

agoraphobia = fear of losing control, freaking out, panicking, and generally making a fool of oneself in public.

Louise looked concerned. "Do we need to know those words?"

"Not even a little bit," I reassured them. "I only told you those words to demonstrate my superior knowledge and to show you that there are a whole bunch of reasons that can be behind *fear of flying*."

Larry yawned and rubbed his eyes—big words sometimes have that effect on people. I reassured them.

"I promise, that's the last time I'll use big words."

The Walkers relaxed. *That's better. It was only a small fib!*

Jane raised her hand. "Felix, I don't know why I am afraid of flying."

"The reasons why are not so important, Jane. Much of your fear is based on stories you have told yourself about flying. If we can clear out some of that rubbish you will be well on your way."

She smiled and nodded.

"Let's get back to the slides. Did you know that you are wired to feel anxiety and fear, and that there is nothing you can do to eliminate it entirely?"

"Nothing?" demanded Larry. "I knew we should have left."

I growled at Larry's outburst, then continued, "They cannot be eliminated, but they can be tamed."

As I gruffly restarted the projector I thought about Larry and his outburst. *I'm going to have problems with that one!*

Lesson 2: Fear and Anxiety

Fear and anxiety are **self-defence mechanisms.** They are designed to make you pay attention to things or situations that might be dangerous to you.

If your body believes you are in danger it will do amazing things to protect itself, without you having to think about it.

Your body does much of your thinking for you.

Anxiety

The caveman in this picture is worried about his safety, although he is not exactly sure why. He is in a "worked-up" state, looking out for danger. This state is called **anxiety**.

His pulse rate quickens and he might be sweating more than usual. He might have a nervous feeling in his stomach or chest. There are a bunch of things the body does to get itself ready for the unknown.

Our brains do this for us automatically.

Feeling anxious may not be fun but it is perfectly normal.

Some anxiety can be a good thing, as it increases our awareness and our "readiness for action." Too much anxiety, however, is not helpful.

Fear - The *Run or Fight* response

If a lion leaps toward the caveman he will experience immediate changes in the way his body works.

A drug called **adrenalin** is released into his blood, quickly travelling throughout his body. Adrenalin makes him, for a short time, **stronger and faster**.

The extra speed helps if he needs to **run,** the extra strength helps if he needs to **fight**. This is called the ***run or fight*** response.

(It is also often called the "fight or flight" response, but that can be confusing when talking about flying!)

Our bodies automatically react this way when we are afraid. You don't have to think about it—it just happens. This is an amazing adaptation of the human body that gives us the best chance of survival in times of great danger.

The problem is: we get this boost of adrenalin when we are afraid of *anything*, even things we can do nothing about.

Fighting or running *will not* solve the problem if we are afraid of flying; adrenalin will not help us to be calm and relaxed.

Yes... You Are Normal!

As we have seen, fear and anxiety are a natural part of life. They are responses that are hard-wired into our bodies by millions of years of evolution. A certain level of anxiety speeds up our reactions and the run-or-fight response protects us from actual danger.

This is an awesome survival instinct. Without it humans would not have survived to become "king monkey."

These instincts can cause a bunch of unpleasant feelings and reactions to *anything* of which we are afraid.

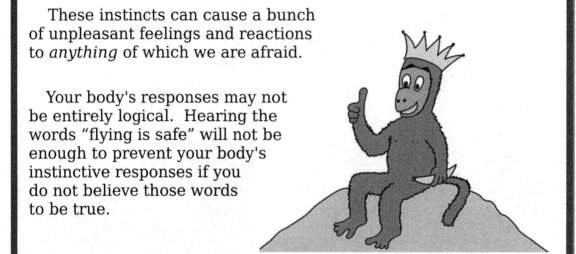

Your body's responses may not be entirely logical. Hearing the words "flying is safe" will not be enough to prevent your body's instinctive responses if you do not believe those words to be true.

Belief **is required, not just words.**

Don't worry! We will address the troublesome issues of flying in ways that will make perfect sense. We will help you believe.

First, however, you will need to learn how your imagination creates the images and stories that terrify you.

Questions About Anxiety

After the second set of slides Larry had a question. "So you are saying that anxiety is a good thing? You've gotta be kidding!"

"*Some* anxiety is a good thing," I replied, "It quickens your responses. Too much, however, will tie you into a knot."

Johnny giggled at the image in his mind of his sister as a pretzel. "That must be why you are so loopy Jane!"

Jane gave him a sideways snarl. "We *all* have too much anxiety, I think. Anxiety grows into fear."

An impressive observation. "Very good, Jane. That *can* happen if anxiety is allowed to grow. Does anyone know how to stop from having any anxiety at all?"

The Walkers, young and old, looked at each other blankly. Larry shrugged his shoulders.

I grinned, "You are quite correct. It is *not possible* to eliminate all anxiety from our lives."

"Then what are we doing here?" asked Louise, disappointed that there was no magic cure.

I explained: "You cannot avoid *all* anxiety, nor can you switch off your 'run-or-fight' response. As a prey animal, these things are wired into your bodies by millions of years of evolution. You can, however, learn to reduce the causes and the unpleasant side effects."

"I guess that will have to do," agreed Larry. Johnny, however, was muttering about wanting to hear more stories of cavemen and fierce creatures.

"What is the matter, little human? Wouldn't you rather learn about how *you* make up your own stories to terrify yourself? That's got to be better than some old caveman tale."

Johnny gave a shrug, then nodded.

"Alright then. Let's continue with the slides and learn how you are *all* amazing storytellers."

Time to restart the projector... "Pay attention now... this next bit is important!"

Lesson 3: Artistry of the Mind

Imagination is a wonderful thing. With it you can create entire worlds and graphic stories of amazing detail—with *you* as the main character.

Your imagination will often amuse and delight you, but it can also cause problems. Your mind will often *invent a story* to match the information you have on a topic. It will do this for you even if your information is incomplete or incorrect.

Your mind automatically "joins the dots" to create a ***virtual reality***, an imaginary world which matches and explains the few things you know.

Your mind and your imagination will create this virtual world whether you want it to or not.

Virtual Reality

Our minds get up to all kinds of tricks, even without our direct permission. For example, what do you see in this diagram?

Most people will see a white triangle.

Of course: *there is no triangle there*. Your mind has *created* the triangle based on a few pieces of information arranged in a particular way.

It is difficult *not* to see this triangle, even if you tell yourself that it is just three dots with pieces cut out.

The triangle is real, as far as your mind is concerned, even though it had to make *assumptions* to fill in the missing parts.

*The triangle is a **virtual reality** made up by your mind to explain the things that it knows. It is **a story** that may, or may not, be the truth.*

In this example your mind created the triangle based on a few known facts. Your brain does this kind of thing for you automatically, often without you noticing.

Whether or not your virtual reality actually represents the truth depends on the quality of the facts upon which it is based.

This can cause problems:

If your "facts" are wrong then the story your mind creates to explain them will be wrong too!

The Perfect Storyteller

Our minds are beautifully designed to create a story to explain anything, and to do this based on a *minimum* of facts.

We have evolved this way.

Back in the time when being eaten was a part of everyday life, a good imagination had real survival benefits.

NO IMAGINATION, EASY PREY

VIVID IMAGINATION, DIFFICULT TO CATCH

An imaginative mind can, by joining the dots of known facts, create a vivid image of danger *without waiting for the full facts to emerge.*

This can be useful but, in the modern world, it is not *always* helpful.

Your Own Movie Projector

The storyteller of your mind creates a virtual reality based upon the "facts" you have about the world. If these "facts" are frightening then your virtual reality can be like a disaster movie, with you as the victim.

Your mind then shows you this movie, over and over.

Have you ever watched a scary movie and felt scared?

Have you ever jumped with fright while watching TV?

A classic horror movie example is the cat that leaps out unexpectedly in a moment of tension.

This *"horror movie cat-effect"* shows that your body reacts to images that are not real. In the same way, your body will respond to images of disaster created by your imagination.

**If the scene in your mind is scary enough,
you _will_ be afraid.**

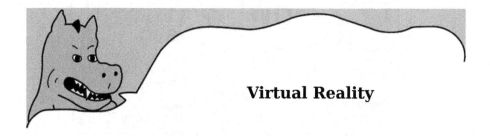

Virtual Reality

**Your imagination creates a picture based
on a few available facts.**

*"If the facts you base your picture on are wrong,
you CANNOT come up with a true picture!"*

Your Body Believes!

If you *believe* that something is dangerous your body will react as if it *really is* that dangerous. You will experience anxiety and fear because of what you believe, even if it is not actually true. Belief is a powerful thing and your body does not care about the facts.

Anxiety will make you tense, worried and on the lookout for any signs of danger.

Fear and the **run or fight** response will quicken your pulse and make you sweat. You may feel clammy, or tight in the stomach. There are many things you may feel because of fear.

The storyteller of your mind is fabulous at creating images of danger based on the few things that you know.

From a few scattered "facts" it may, if you allow it, fill in the missing parts with gory and frightening details.

Your imagination may create a horror movie—with you starring as the victim!

This story is largely a work of fiction, and yet...

You believe, so your body reacts as if it was real!

What Picture of Flying Do You Have?

The storyteller of your mind may have created a frightening image of flying.

In the same way that you invented a triangle based on three dots, your mind may have invented a fearful story based on a few unpleasant "facts", ideas and memories, *and made the rest up!*

In this picture in your head you might see flying as

- Dangerous
- Scary
- Unpleasant
- Stupid

Everyone's image is different. Only *you* will know what picture your mind has created.

What is *your* image of flying?

*Is your picture of flying REAL,
or is it a dragon created out of thin air?*

Automatic Responses

I turned off the projector.

"Your brain invents a story to fit your facts and your body responds automatically. Any questions?"

Johnny, who was clearly interested in gadgets, asked "Dragon, can I get one of those virtual reality headsets?"

I smiled. "They are available in the Fear Dragons Gift Shop, but you really don't need one. Your brain *is* a virtual reality headset that requires no batteries!"

"Bollocks," guffed Larry. "There is no way that is true. I know how the world works. I know the truth when I see it."

"Did you see the white triangle?"

"Yeah, of course. So what?"

"And did you understand the bit about the *horror-movie cat effect* — the way your body reacts to something scary automatically?"

Larry shook his head. "I saw it, but I *don't* believe it."

Clearly, some people take more convincing than others. "Come close, Larry. I have a secret to tell you."

Despite already knowing everything, Larry stood and stepped forward. I leaned close enough to whisper in Larry's ear.

Instead of whispering, however, I opened my gaping jaws as if to bite Larry's head off, and ROARRRED. Needless to say, Larry jumped.

Then I backed away, closed my jaws and smiled. Larry and his family stared in shock and horror. They had *all* jumped in fright at my demonstration.

"O-O-Okay Felix. I g-g-et it," said Larry, who had discovered some automatic bodily reactions he found quite uncomfortable.

It may be said that the things dragons find funny are not always fully appreciated by humans. That did not concern me, however; I let go a full belly laugh and pointed at the dishevelled Larry.

"Got you a beauty, eh lad?"

Strangely, however, my valued clients did not seem to be sharing my enjoyment. In fact, they seemed quite tense.

Like all dragons, I was sensitive to these things. I noticed that their heart rates were elevated, that they were breathing shallowly and quickly, and that they were sweating. There was also a strange and unpleasant smell coming from Larry.

"Perhaps we'd better take a time-out from the questions. How about we continue the slides and then practice some relaxation techniques?"

No reply or obvious enthusiasm flowed from the Walkers, who were still in shock.

"Before I continue," I asked, "does anyone else have a problem believing in their own automatic responses to fear? I could tell you another secret..."

"NO!" the Walkers cried in unison.

"Okay, okay." I restarted the projector for the next set of slides. *Best to keep moving and put this unpleasant episode behind us!*

Lesson 4: Mind Weather

Your emotional state is like the weather: sometimes it is calm and sunny; at other times it is stormy, gloomy and unpleasant. Anxiety is the "wet and windy" kind of mind weather.

Unlike real weather, however, we can influence the meteorology of the mind. There are steps that we can take to calm the stormy skies inside our heads.

Sometimes your mind does a great job of convincing itself to be afraid. We have discussed some reasons why this occurs.

For example, your mind will use the few "facts" it has on a topic and make the rest up.

This can result in miserable mind weather. You may experience weather effects such as:

- Churning guts
- Increased pulse and tight chest
- Slight breathlessness
- Sweating or clamminess
- Uncomfortable bowel or bladder

Relax! Forecast: Fine Weather Ahead

It is easy to *say* "relax" but is it possible to do? Sometimes our minds and bodies do not want to give up their tension easily. Relaxation is a skill you can practice, so that you become tension's master rather than its slave. There are many techniques that can help.

It should come as no surprise that your body and mind are closely related. Deep breathing techniques rely on this fact, to calm your mind by controlling one of the physical symptoms of anxiety and fear.

Deep Breathing Exercise 1

Try breathing deeply and *slowly*, focussing on your breath. Keep doing this for a while, slowly counting in your head while you do it (if this helps).

IN ...ONE, ...TWO, ...THREE (pause)

OUT ...ONE ...TWO ...THREE (pause)

IN ...ONE, ...TWO, ...THREE (pause)...

After a short time you will feel more relaxed and notice that your pulse rate has slowed.

It makes sense that this would work. When you are *nervous* or *anxious* (*not* relaxed), your pulse and breathing rates increase. It has been observed that this process works in reverse. Slow your breathing and you will slow your pulse rate—and feel more relaxed.

In Lesson 2 we discussed *anxiety*, a state in which your mind is on high alert, actively looking for danger.

When you are anxious your imagination can run amok. The dragon in your mind loves amok!

If you can relax
you will keep your fear dragon away.

We will discuss another variation of this deep breathing technique shortly, but there are many other relaxation techniques that can help.

Read some books on relaxation, or visit a psychologist, relaxation therapist or Buddhist for help with relaxation techniques.   Relaxing is an excellent strategy and the more you practice the better at it you will get.

TIP: When feeling tense, saying the word "relax" to yourself and taking a deep breath can focus your awareness and help you to relax.

The Tension Tornado

Your mind does not stop just because it has created a virtual reality for you to believe in; it will continue to gather more information. The natural tendency of your mind is to assume that the story it has already created is the truth, so any new information will be used, if possible, to support the existing story.

Your mind may, therefore, use your own physical symptoms of anxiety as proof that there is something to be anxious about. This is a circular argument that defies logic—but we are human; not everything about us is entirely logical.

In this circular argument your mind uses your anxiety symptoms as proof of danger. Your mind is saying to itself: "I feel these things so there *must* be something to be afraid of!"

This results in an *increase* in anxiety and fear; it also, therefore, results in an increase in your symptoms. These worsening symptoms may then be used as further proof, and the situation can spiral out of control. This results in a perfect storm!

I AM TENSE SO I SHOULD BE...

ANXIOUS SO I SHOULD BE

AFRAID SO I SHOULD

PANIC!

The Tension Tornado

Stop the Tornado

If you feel yourself being drawn into an emotional tornado you can do something about it. This is easiest if you get in early, before the storm gathers strength, but it can be done at any time.

Stopping the tornado is a two-step process:

1. **Awareness** — notice that you are not calm.
2. **Stop** what you are doing or thinking, so that the storm cannot feed on itself.

Step 1: Awareness. (Hey, I Don't Feel Calm!)

The first step in avoiding a tornado is to realise that you are being drawn into one; you have to realise that you are not calm before you can decide to do something about it.

Sometimes your "fear meter" seems to move all by itself!

You may not have an actual "fear meter," but you can rely on your own body and feelings to give you indications. You simply need to be aware of the signs.

You will have your own list of symptoms—things that your body does when you are tense or anxious. These are early warning signs, indications that your own "fear meter" is being pulled toward the dark side of anxiety, fear and panic.

It does not matter *why* this is occurring. Recognising that you are not calm enables you to do something about it. If you can address these feelings and symptoms then you can pull yourself back toward calm. If you can **stop** your current thinking and relax then you will stop the tornado from developing.

If you notice yourself being drawn away
from calm, ***do something about it!***

Step 2: Stop! (Don't Let The Storm Feed on Itself)

When you notice that you are not calm and your anxiety seems to be increasing, STOP!

Stop what you are doing, and what you are thinking. They are obviously not helping you to be calm. Try, instead, to take a relaxing "time-out."

Anything that you find relaxing or mentally diverting may help get your mind out of the spiral path.

Relaxation is the friend of calm.

Deep Breathing Exercise 2

We have already suggested one simple deep breathing relaxation technique. Here is another which includes some words to help get you out of a fearful frame of mind:

STOP, BREATHE, LET GO, THINK SAFE

1. STOP what you are doing.

2. BREATHE IN, deeply and slowly

3. Breathe out, saying "LET GO"

4. Say, "I AM SAFE"

Repeat this breathing exercise until you can THINK SAFE.

There are many other relaxation techniques you can try, and many books and CDs are available on the subject. Give them a try, and see what works for you.

Stretching feels great and relaxes the mind and body!

A Relaxing Break

The Walkers seemed relaxed after their deep breathing. I remembered that humans have short attention spans, so I figured this was a good time for a break.

"We've covered some good ground so far. How about I make you a nice cup of Decaf Darjeeling and a pineapple juice for the kids?"

As she was enjoying her tea in the tearoom, Louise asked, "What's the deal with the *Tension Tornado?* I can't imagine why our bodies are wired up that way. What purpose does it serve?"

"Good question Louise. Not everything in our bodies is useful; take my appendix, please. There may, however, be a good reason your body is designed this way. You are designed to respond quickly to the first hint of danger. That gives you the best chance to avoid being eaten."

"Yes, but what does that have to do with the tornado?"

"Maybe your body observes its own reactions to allow it to react more quickly. This is called a 'positive feedback system', which can provide the quickest responses. The side effect, if you let it occur, is tension that feeds on itself. Then the tornado forms and you end up in a panic!"

"But we really don't want to panic, do we?"

"Panic is never beneficial. It results in poor decision making. Look at what happens to panicked shoppers late on Christmas Eve—they buy all sorts of junk. For example, check out this crazy-face tie that someone gave me last year. Unbelievable!"

"So what can we do?" asked Louise.

"Shop early. Oh, you mean about the tornado? Whenever you feel tense or anxious, do something to stop it. Relaxation, or diversion, will get you out of the spin cycle."

Jane joined the conversation. "Felix, I've tried the things that you suggest but they just don't seem to work."

The other Walkers nodded in agreement, except for Johnny who was trying to get a candy bar out of the vending machine without paying.

I sipped my tea while thinking about these questions.

No single answer is going to suit everybody, as I explained:

"Everyone is different and you will have to experiment to find what works for you. When you feel yourself being drawn into anxiety and beyond, here's some things you could try:

- Listen to some relaxing music.
- Have a quiet lie down.
- Stretch and relax your muscles. Be aware of which parts of your body are tense and focus on relaxing those muscles.
- Do some exercise.
- Repeat in your own mind a chant like 'I am safe' or 'It will pass'. It will and you know it.
- Make yourself a cuppa but stay away from caffeine. Caffeine gives you some of the same body responses as anxiety and will not help."

Time was getting along, so I collected their cups.

"Let's go back to the presentation room. We've still got a lot of ground to cover, and time waits for no dragon."

PART TWO

Beliefs

Lesson 5: Changing Your Beliefs

Sometimes fears are based on incorrect beliefs. Your mind uses these to create a **story**, or an **image,** that is not true but is something that *you believe is true.*

The image you have formed in your mind may include misunderstandings, half-truths and lies.

If your mind is using incorrect beliefs as building blocks the story it will create to explain them may be fearsome. Such an image may be far worse than reality. A dragon is born!

There is good news, however. Your "dragon," a fearsome story based on incorrect facts and beliefs, will cease to exist if you get your facts straight. Sort out your beliefs and the image will fade.

> ***If you get your "facts" straight***
> ***then your mind will not jump to***
> ***wrong conclusions so quickly.***

For example, rearranging the information in our picture makes it more difficult to invent the imaginary triangle in the middle:

In the same way, if we can sort out our beliefs about flying our storytelling mind will be less likely to come up with a frightening explanation.

Replace incorrect "facts" with truth!

In the next lessons we will talk about some of the incorrect facts your mind may be using, and then we'll add some truths to the image. Your dragon will have to find somewhere else to live!

Grand Pronouncements

Sometimes the best way to start a discussion about an important topic is to make a grand pronouncement, and I thought a costume would help. While the Walkers were watching the slideshow I had ducked up to my office; I returned wearing a toga.

I paused the slides and stood in front of the screen, held my head high, and cleared my throat...

Projecting my voice across the vast auditorium—or storeroom, depending on your point of view—I spoke as Senator Felix addressing the Roman government:

"Friends, Romans, countrymen, lend me your fears!"

I had thought that stealing a line from Shakespeare was quite clever but my students seemed confused. Perhaps it was the toga. I tried another grand pronouncement:

"Beliefs are the cause, and the cure, of fear!"

Vacant stares were returned from my audience. *Tough crowd!* I lowered the tone of my voice and pronounced, forebodingly:

"Lies beget lies!"

Louise, who thought that a 'beget' was a French breadstick, asked, "What are you on, dragon?"

"I, dear lady, am a master of disguise, illusion and subterfuge! I can play your emotions and your fear like a musical instrument. Your lives are but a theatre for my own amusement!"

Louise crossed her arms. "Felix, do you really believe that rubbish?"

"Well, I thought it sounded pretty good." My pronouncements had not had the effect I had intended. I expected applause and a vigorous discussion, but instead received abuse and disbelief.

It would clearly take more than just grand pronouncements to shift the Walkers' beliefs.

"I'll tell you what, Louise. I am going to show you how we work around here. I will take you into the shadowy world of the Fear Dragons. You will see how we help *you* to build a house of lies, a place for your fear to live well and grow fat!"

Larry, who had already seen one of my "secrets" and didn't like it, looked concerned.

"Relax, Larry. You needn't worry. It is reasonably safe."

I was enjoying the opportunity for some theatrics, so I switched back to my senatorial voice and again addressed the crowd:

"The only thing you have to fear is fear itself!"

The great thing about a toga is it hides the fact that you've put on a couple of pounds and it is possible that some of my other costumes would have disturbed them more. For example, here is a picture of one of my other favourites:

As I thought about which costume might have worked better it occurred to me that no matter how you dress up a grand pronouncement it, alone, will not shift beliefs.

Some ideas, however, do take root in people's minds when they are dressed up as "facts."

I restarted the projector. The next topic was one of the most important that would help the Walkers understand how their own stories are distorted into something fearful. I talk, of course, about Lies, the favourite tool of the Fear Dragon.

Felix's Most Unusual
FEAR OF FLYING COURSE
SLIDE PRESENTATION

Lesson 6: Lies

There are lots of ideas about flying that are not true. Some of those ideas become a part of your own story about flying.

To eliminate the "dragon" in your mind you will need to find these untrue ideas and replace them with something more useful.

Many of the things told to us are lies. Some people may lie deliberately, for their own reasons. Others think that they are telling us the truth, but they are actually only passing on lies they heard from somebody else. Sometimes we lie to ourselves.

Our fears grow well when fed by lies. Let's talk about some of the "porkies" that people tell, and believe, about flying.

Lie #1: The wings will snap off!

This is a lie that you tell to yourself, either in words or by imagining a disaster scene in which it happens.

An aeroplane's wings are unbelievably strong. They are designed to handle huge amounts of force—far more than they will ever experience in real life.

They are also designed to be flexible, allowing them to bend and bounce in turbulence. This looks freaky, but it is an important part of what makes them so incredibly strong.

The wings will never break off. If you think that they will then you have created a dragon in your mind. How many planes do you think Boeing and Airbus would sell if the wings could break off?

***Designing planes that do this would be
BAD FOR BUSINESS!***

For more information about turbulence, check out Lesson 10 on page 115. You will see that it is no big deal.

Lie #2: Planes crash all the time (I saw it on TV!)

This is a lie told to you by others. Did you know that most "news" services are in the business of making you afraid?

The "news" is about telling stories that people *want* to hear. The news providers want to sell more papers, or get more people watching their TV shows. They *love* scary stories.

They know that many people are afraid of flying, so any story about an aeroplane problem will be made into *big* news. Their stories are made as scary as possible, even if nobody was hurt; words like "plummet" and "crash" are used when "rapid descent" and "rough landing" would do. Maybe that's why they're called "news *stories*," rather than "news facts."

Actually, if you take **2 flights every month** you could expect, on average, to be accident-free for **50,000 years*.** Not bad, but you won't hear this statistic on the news— it isn't scary enough.

* Source: International Air Transport Association (IATA),
aircraft accidents 1 per 1.2 million flights (2007)

Lie #3: Terrorists Are Waiting For Me To Fly

Despite what the "news" people want you to believe, *not everyone in the world is out to get you.*

At times, the news coverage of events would have us thinking that everyone who dresses a certain way is a terrorist. This is not true.

Occasionally, of course, cranky people have caused problems on aeroplanes.

This is *very* rare and we have learned some excellent ways to discourage these troublemakers. Security checkpoints are just one part of this; there are many more security measures behind the scenes, and air travel is safer now than it has ever been.

The "news" services are one group that benefit if you are continually worried about terrorists—fear sells lots of newspapers and news-show advertising. They will sometimes, therefore, magnify and multiply terrorism related stories.

Airport Security Officers Pat Medown & Ray Bann

By repeatedly showing the most graphic images, and by talking about terrorism in such a way as it seems that *you* are next on the hit list, these "news entertainers" are messing with your mind. It is their *magnification* of the problem that is the lie.

Nothing is as simple as the news shows tell you, and there is not a terrorist under every rock.

> ***Believe it or not, terrorists have more to worry about than stalking <u>you</u>!***

The security checkpoint is always good fun!

Lie #4: I *Must* Panic When I Fly!!!

Some people tell themselves that they *will* panic if they fly.

> *A **panic attack** is a sudden period of intense fear or extreme anxiety, and is simply the "run or fight response" in action.*

If you've ever had a panic attack you may be worried that it will happen again. You may, then, tell yourself a lie:

"I will freak-out if I fly"

This is a lie because: **panic is not compulsory!**

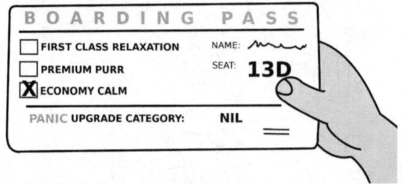

Many people will have a panic attack sometime in their lives, and avoiding places where panic might reoccur is a common response.

It takes time to regain trust in yourself. Gradual exposure to problem situations, and learning that flying is harmless, will grow your confidence.

Fear of Flying courses can help, especially if they have access to real aircraft and simulators. These courses allow you to become familiar with the flying experience while remaining firmly on the ground. See the Dragon Slayers section at the end of this book for further information.

There is no rule which says that you must panic.
Don't talk yourself into it!

Lie #5: The Plane Will Crash _Because_ I'm Onboard

Some people tell themselves the story that their plane will crash *because* they have chosen to fly.

They might not put it exactly like that; rather, "It doesn't matter which plane I go on, I will choose the doomed one."

Another way of putting this lovely lie:

> **"*Whichever* choice I make will result in catastrophe."**

Every straw is a short straw when you play with the dragon!

> **For this to be true, the <u>entire Universe</u>
> would have to have been created
> <u>specifically</u> as a trap for YOU.
> This is unlikely.**

Your Story...

What troubles YOU about flying?

(make a list and number them in order of importance)

....

....

....

....

....

....

....

....

....

....

....

....

....

....

Now ask yourself:

Are these stories true, or are they lies that you have chosen to believe?

Discussion About Lies

During the *Lies* slideshow I got rid of the toga and, when the presentation had finished, turned off the projector. "Does anyone have any questions about Lies? Of course, I can't guarantee that I'll give you an honest answer."

Larry was curious. "The slides talked about different kinds of lies: those told to us by others, and those we tell ourselves. Which are the worst?"

"That is an excellent question. Your fear relies on you believing that something is dangerous. It doesn't matter whether it actually is, or is not. If you *believe* that it is dangerous then your body will respond. At the end of the day, it is the lies inside your own head that cause the damage."

Jane observed, "So what is the problem with lies told to us? We don't have to believe them."

"Precisely, Jane, but most humans choose to believe what they are told. When you are surrounded by lies it can be difficult to see the truth. It often seems easiest to believe what we are told, but beware: believing in lies can cause you problems later."

Louise, who had heard her share of lies, asked, "How come you know so much about lies, Felix?"

"It is part of my job. I'm not always a *Fear of Flying* course presenter, you know. I am a Fear Dragon. My job is to create fear, and lies are one of my most important tools."

That didn't make sense to Larry. "Then why are you presenting this course? Why are you helping us, rather than making our fear worse?"

That is the question, isn't it? I smiled, "Because it is my day off! Today I am here to help you."

I had an idea that might make things clearer. "Let's go for a tour of the building, and I'll show you some of the things we do around here. That may help you to understand how fear is made, and how believing in lies is part of the process."

They agreed, and followed me out of the storeroom to the lift which would take us to the upper levels.

BASEMENT
DEPARTMENTS
- CLAUSTROPHOBIA
- THE DARK
- SPIDERS
- COCKROACHES
- MICE AND RATS

———
- TEA ROOM
- STORE
FEAR OF FLYING COURSE

After leaving the lift we passed several doors, with labels such as Fear of Open Spaces, Fear of Otters, and Fear of Ventriloquist Dolls. All of these doors were closed and, as Larry discovered when he rattled the knobs, locked. The door to the Fear of Heights department, however, was slightly ajar.

Louise was tempted to peek inside, but I would not hear of it. "You don't need to look in there. That is a different fear for a different day. Let's solve the *Fear of Flying* first, and you may find that other fears takes care of themselves."

Johnny, lagging behind due to the shortness of his legs, caught up with the others. "Where are you taking us? Are we nearly there?"

"Yes, Johnny, we are nearly there. I'm taking you to see my TV recording studio. I have lots of fun there. You will find it interesting."

"You have a TV studio? Wow! That's cool!"

"We have several studios. We also have radio broadcasting studios, and printing presses for newspapers and magazines."

We passed other doors, such as Fear of Cracks In The Pavement, Fear of Suffocation, and Fear of Turtles.

Eventually we arrived at our destination: Recording Studio Five.

"Here we are! Come on in and I'll show you how I make the news."

"How *you* make the news?" blurted Larry, disbelievingly.

"You betcha," I replied. The Walkers were gobsmacked when I showed them the complex apparatus which allowed me to spread fear via the News.

Enjoying myself with my gadgetry, the Walkers laughed as I made the newsreader tell a story about airline food being poisonous. They particularly liked the puppet-jerky gagging motion of the highly-strung newsreader.

"I love this stuff and it is so easy. The best part is that people seem to think that the news can be trusted. Sometimes yes, sometimes no. The quickest way for a lie to become a belief is when it is spread by a trusted source."

Jane asked a very good question. "Is all news false?"

"No, of course not. But when they are using the words of fear, when they are dwelling on the images of terror, when they are making you afraid: it is *me* pulling the strings!"

Larry and Louise prided themselves on keeping informed by watching the news every night. They were aghast at the revelation about how the news shows are really made. They had not realised how their emotions were being played by the media.

Satisfied that the Walkers had understood this lesson, I put the puppet away. "Enough of that fun. I brought the projector. Let me set it up and we'll watch some more slides. No avoiding the hard work just because we're having a jolly excursion!"

TRY THIS EXPERIMENT NEXT TIME YOU WATCH THE NEWS:

Make some notes about each story in the news show. **Make note of:**

Topic: *What is the story about?*

Emotion: *What did you feel?*

Key Words: *One or two words that were used to help create that emotion.*

How many stories deliberately tried to create or amplify an emotional response?

Lesson 7: Air is Real

Maybe you don't *really* believe that the air can hold an aeroplane up in the sky. *Some kind of magic <u>must</u> be involved!*

You don't have this problem with other forms of transport. For example, it is easy to see what holds a car off the ground:

*Four anti-gravity devices keep
the metal off the road!*

You can even believe that a huge ship made of steel can float...

... because of your early experiences with floating objects.

It may seem, however, that *air is different*. It is difficult to believe in something you cannot see.

**Your early experiments with flight may have been
unsuccessful (and difficult to explain!)**

Perhaps you do not *believe* that air can hold you up in the sky. It *must* be some kind of hocus-pocus!

Let's talk about the air. We will demonstrate that air has the power to make you fly. No magic is required!

Respect for the Air

The slideshow made the point that some people may have a natural distrust of the air's ability to hold them up in the sky.

Larry was in complete agreement with that sentiment. "I remember jumping off the bed wearing a cape and my underpants when I was a kid. It didn't go well!"

Smiling at the thought I replied, "Maybe you just don't trust the air any more Larry. You really should, you know. You breathe the stuff several times a minute; the air has been pretty good to you."

"Yes, but I can't even see it. How am I to believe?"

I pointed up at the sky. "The air is as the sea, the earth, and the fire. It is one of the fundamental elements. Learn its secrets and it will hold you aloft."

Larry replied, "That sounds like hocus-pocus, dragon. I am a man of science."

"Me too, Larry, me too. There are good reasons why you could not fly from the end of your bed. There are fashion reasons—wearing your underpants on the outside is never a good look—but there are scientific reasons too."

As our discussion had turned towards science I figured that perhaps there was a better location for our discussion, so I made a suggestion to my students. "I've got an idea. Let me take you to see our science labs. Science can be used to scare people, but it does have positive uses too. Let's go there to continue our discussion about air."

I led the Walkers down a long corridor. We passed many doors, such as Fear of Commitment, Fear of Missing A Bargain, and Fear of Being Alone. I explained, as we walked, the difficulties for Fear Dragons in creating so many fears. "All of these departments compete for funding. My money is on the Being Alone department; the others seem unable to stick to a budget."

Up in an elevator and then down another corridor, we walked past other departments, including Fear of Global Warming, Fear of Aging, Fear of Germs and Fear of Atomic War.

Johnny ran ahead, stopping in front of a door that was different from the others we had passed. "Hey Felix! Can we take a look in here?"

"Shhh," I said as I caught up. We were standing outside the very creepy Politically Incorrect Fears Department and I did not want to hang around.

Just loud enough for the Walkers to hear, I explained, "I never liked this place. Those guys dealt with some very unpleasant fears over the years. The dragons who worked there were a little... strange."

STOP!
THIS AREA IS CLASSIFIED

BS4

"What do they do in there, Felix?" asked Louise.

"Nothing now... its been shut down. But their past projects included Religious Intolerance, Racism and Prejudice."

The Walkers had a look of disgust on their faces.

"Yes, I know," said Felix. "It is ridiculous and I'm glad Fear Dragons have nothing to do with that stuff any more. These days those fears are created only by humans."

We kept walking and, rounding a curved part of the corridor, found ourselves standing in front of a double door prominently labelled "Fear Dragons Laboratories." I invited them inside.

"Welcome to our Science Department. This is one of the largest departments at Fear Dragons. It is a combined department, some work being done to make people afraid of science, and some actual scientific experiments."

"How do you make people afraid of science?" asked Larry.

"Have you heard of the Hadron Collider?"

"I have," said Jane. "It is going to create a black hole that will suck up the Earth."

I winked and let them in on a secret. "That fear was one of ours!"

It was time for me to do some serious science, so I donned a white lab coat and found some chairs for the Walkers. I gathered some ingredients and set up my apparatus at one of the chemistry benches.

As I worked I must have been content, as I was humming an old Christmas tune that reminded me of happy days.

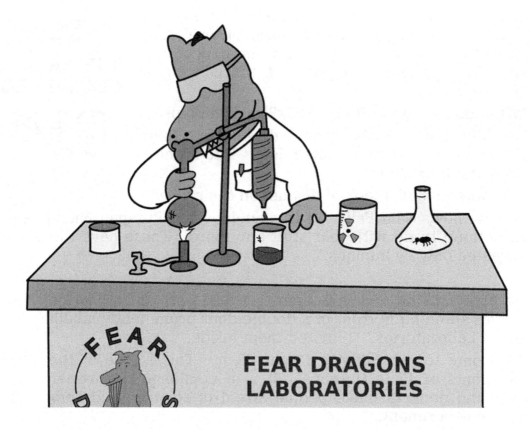

No doubt the Walkers were curious, but I was off in a world of my own, remembering my girlfriend Foxy who had taught me this recipe. Johnny asked, "What are you making, Felix? Fear potion?"

"Nope. I'm making a *Dragonfire Sling*. I learned the recipe at our Christmas party last year. They're quite good; perfectly harmless. I'll give you a taste, if you like."

Seeing that the ingredients included spiders and uranium they shuddered and declined. *No accounting for taste!*

"In that case, let me set up the projector again and you can watch some more slides. You'll learn of a very interesting scientific experiment that will help you believe in the air."

I took a sip of my spicy cocktail—*just right!*—and chuckled, thinking of Larry leaping off his bed dressed as a superhero.

"Some things, my friends, you simply have to try."

Lesson 8: A Very Dangerous Experiment

In this Lesson we will show you a very simple science experiment which demonstrates *exactly* how wings keep a plane in the sky.

I must warn you: this experiment is very dangerous. We are trained professionals, conducting this experiment in a controlled environment. Do **not** try this in your home.

Warning!

This experiment involves sticking your hand out of the window of a moving car. This may be ILLEGAL in some countries, and should only ever be done where safe and with the permission of the driver of the car.

*Science Officer
"Thrust" Master*

THIS EXPERIMENT SHOULD <u>ONLY</u> BE DONE IN A CONTROLLED ENVIRONMENT... NOT ON PUBLIC ROADS, AND WITH NO OBSTRUCTIONS OR OTHER VEHICLES ANYWHERE NEARBY!

WARNING:
Sticking your hand out the window
of a car has certain risks!

The Experiment:
Feel the Lift

In this experiment you will:

* Feel the power of **lift**
* Learn how the **angle** of a wing determines **lift** and **drag**.
* Learn how the **speed** of a wing affects the lift produced.

First, some definitions:

LIFT:
the UPWARDS force produced by a wing, which lifts an aeroplane from the ground.

DRAG:
the *"wind-in-your-face* slow-you-down" force.

Background to the experiment:

An aeroplane's wings are just like two planks of wood. As the aeroplane moves through the air they are positioned by the pilots to make an angle to the air, so as to deflect air downwards. This creates the lift the plane needs to fly.

We will experiment with moving a plank-like object through the air to see what happens. We will also try varying the angle that the plank-like thing makes with the air, and the speed at which it moves through that air.

Now, I just need to find something resembling a plank of wood. Ah, Captain, you will do nicely!

Step 1: Stick your hand out the window, flat.

The first part of this experiment is to hold your hand flat, like a plank of wood, out the window of a car.

When the car is moving, and *if it is safe to do so*, put your hand out the window, keeping it perfectly flat so all of your fingers are at the same height.

REMEMBER: Sticking your hand out the window of a car can be dangerous. Heed the warnings!

Can you feel your hand being blown back slightly?

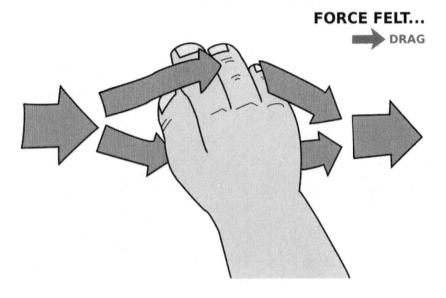

FORCE FELT...
➡ DRAG

- Because you are moving through the air, it feels like a wind is blowing. Faster the car, the stronger the wind.

- With your hand flat the wind splits equally, some passing above and some below your hand.

- The wind has **not** been *deflected* (changed direction) so your hand is not lifted up.

- You will feel a slight push backwards as the wind tries to blow your hand back. This force is called ***drag***.

Step 2: Twist your hand to make an angle with the air

Twist your hand so that the forward edge of your hand is higher than the rear edge (your thumb higher than your "pinky").

Can you feel your hand being lifted up?

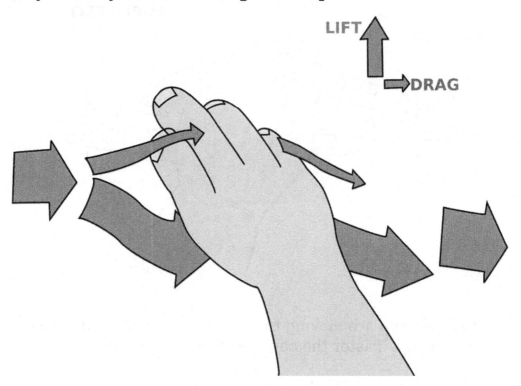

- The wind that you feel is the same as before...
- ... but this time most of that wind is *deflected downward.*
- Because you are pushing the air downward you will feel an opposite force pushing your hand *upward.*
- This upward force is called **lift.** This is the magic which makes planes fly. Simple, eh?

You will also notice the **drag** force has increased, pushing your hand back. You will have to exert some effort to hold your hand out straight to prevent it being blown back.

Step 3: Vary your "hand angle"

You will notice that the greater the angle of your hand, the greater the lift force you feel. This is because you are deflecting the wind in a more downwards direction, so you get a stronger upwards opposite force.

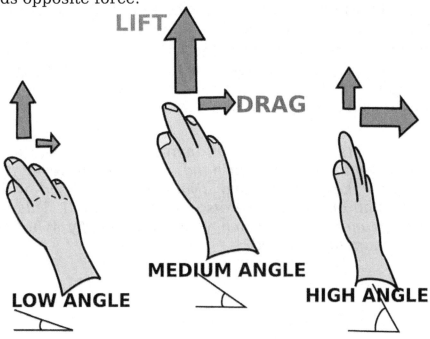

LIFT

DRAG

MEDIUM ANGLE

LOW ANGLE

HIGH ANGLE

GREATER HAND ANGLE = GREATER LIFT

This works up to a point. Beyond a certain angle you will actually feel less lift, as the air is no longer cleanly deflected. It is, instead, being "churned" by your hand. As you continue to increase your hand angle the lift will decrease further.

In technical terms, when your hand angle is high enough to notice the decrease in lift, your hand-wing is "stalled." There is still lift produced, but not as much, and there is a lot more drag.

Challenge: Try to "fly" your hand. Experiment to find the hand angle which will exactly support the weight of your hand at your current speed.

Step 4: Different speeds.

Try this experiment with the car moving at different speeds.

Faster: At a faster speed, more air is deflected for a given hand angle, resulting in more lift. To reduce the amount of lift to what you felt previously, reduce your hand-angle.

Slower: As the car goes slower, the wind blowing over your hand is slower so less lift is produced for any given hand angle. To keep enough lift to support your hand you must increase the angle your hand makes with the wind.

As the car gets slower, you can increase the angle to maintain the lift required to support your hand. Too slow, however, and you can no longer keep your hand flying, as your hand will have passed the stall angle that we discovered in Step 3. This defines the <u>minimum</u> airspeed at which your hand will fly. What is your hand's minimum flight speed?

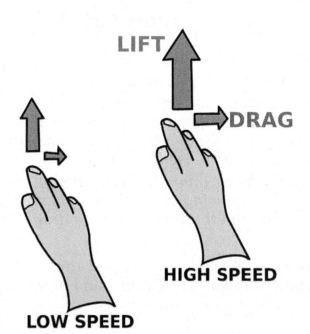

For the same lift (to exactly support the weight of your hand):

- High Speed needs Low hand angle

- Low Speed needs High hand angle

Discussion: What Does This Have To Do With Aeroplanes?

This experiment shows exactly the way an aeroplane wing works. The pilots control the amount of lift by controlling the angle that the wings meet the air and the speed of the aircraft. They do this to get exactly the lift that they need (and, you'll be happy to know, it is easier than it sounds!)

Why don't planes have hands instead of wings?

By making wings a particular shape we can get *more* lift and *less drag* than if we used giant hands. That's why aeroplanes have wings instead of hands, but they lift the aeroplane up in just the same way.

In this experiment we have shown, in a simple way, how wings work. It is the wings which provide the lift that keeps a plane flying. The engines overcome the drag force, keeping us moving through the sky, but it is the wings which do the lifting.

It is worthwhile trying this experiment for yourself, because *feeling is believing.* You cannot see the air, but by feeling the power of lift on your own hand, you will believe:

> ### The wings will work every time;
> ### magic is not required!

Distrust of Machines

After the Science Experiment slideshow Johnny asked his father, "Can we try that experiment Dad?"

"Sure, Johnny."

To make sure that I would not get sued if they lost their hands conducting the experiment, I reminded them, "Make sure you heed the safety warnings! Otherwise you will be quite armless!"

I chuckled to myself. *I really was the wittiest dragon in the room!*

Louise also had a question about the slides. "I thought it was the engines that made a plane fly. You're saying it is the wings?"

"Yes," I replied, "and that experiment proves it. All the engines do is push you through the air, overcoming the drag force that you would feel slowing you down, but it is the wings that make it fly."

"What if the engines stop working? What will happen then?"

"The plane will glide! Have you ever made a model glider or a paper plane? They have no engines. A well designed one can fly really well."

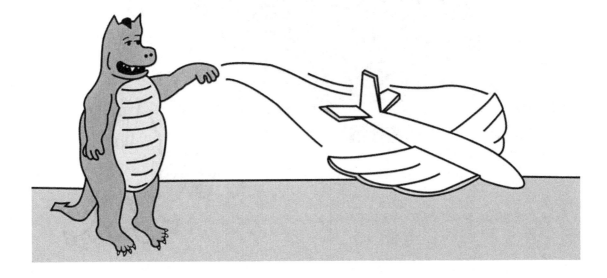

Larry said, "The engines are just one part of a plane, Louise. There are thousands of parts in a plane that can break, and if any part breaks, you are doomed!"

I couldn't help chuckling. "You don't trust machines, do you Larry?"

"No, not really. Why are you laughing?"

"Can I let you in on another of my secrets? One reason that you don't trust aeroplanes is because of my one-on-one work with you in the past. I have laid the groundwork for your distrust of machines."

"What are you talking about, dragon?"

"I have taught you, over the years, that machines will let you down. For example, I made your lawnmower hard to start. I have made your car break down at very inconvenient times. Even the bus that you then had to catch to work broke down, didn't it?"

Larry nodded. All of these things had happened.

"And who do you think caused your DVD player to stop working two days after the warranty expired?" I asked with a smug look on my face.

Larry growled.

I smiled and waved. "Yep. Me again!"

Johnny jumped to his feet, vindicated. "See, Dad! I told you it wasn't me that broke it!"

"What's the point telling us this?" grumbled Louise, who had also had several machines let her down, particularly the cheap, low quality things they occasionally bought to save money.

"You think a plane is just like these other machines. You think, because of your experiences with other machines letting you down, that a plane will break down and fall from the sky."

I continued, getting to the important bit. "Here's the news: A modern airliner is different. It is designed differently and it is built differently. That's what the next set of slides is about.

"Maybe after the next section you will have trouble remembering what it was that made you so afraid of planes."

Felix's Most Unusual
FEAR OF FLYING COURSE
SLIDE PRESENTATION

Lesson 9: Planes Are Safe

If your car breaks down you can pull over to the side of the road, make a phone call, and wait until the repair truck arrives.

Of course, you cannot do this in an aeroplane.

You should not be concerned about this; aeroplanes are designed very differently from cars.

Over the next few slides we will discuss how aeroplanes are designed, and how we look after them. You will see why:

***Airliners are the safest form of
public transport ever designed.***

- 105 -

Lessons We Have Learned...

We have learned, since coming down from the trees, that machines break down from time to time.

All machines break down eventually.

We have also learned that machines will not let us down if:

1. They are good **quality** (*well designed and well made*)

2. We **treat them well**   (*well trained crew*)

3. We **repair** them when necessary (*maintenance*)

And, just in case things do break down:

4. It is good to have a **spare**   (*redundancy*)

Quality

A quality machine is one which has been very carefully designed and manufactured.

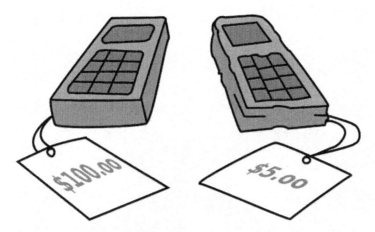

Which phone would you expect to be of higher quality?

It is generally true that a high quality machine costs more than a low quality machine.

Airliners are very expensive. A small jet might cost $50 million dollars, while a big four-engine jumbo might cost in excess of $300 million. *None* are cheap!

The high price tag should assure you that:

Modern airliners are of the <u>highest</u> quality!

Well Trained Crew Treat Their Machines Well

The pilots of a quality airline are professionals. They have made it their life's work to become very good at what they do.

They know how to look after your aeroplane, and how to get the most from it. Operating your aircraft safely and well is a source of quiet pride for aviators.

Maintenance...
Repair When Necessary

The engineers of a quality airline pride themselves on how they look after their aeroplanes.

Engineer Mel says:

"This is my life's work. There is nothing I do not know, or cannot find out, about your plane. I know how to fix any gremlin that pops up.

"We inspect your plane before *every* flight, topping up the oils and checking the tyres. We will fix anything that need fixing *when* it needs fixing. Be assured, we will not allow your plane to fly if it is not in good condition."

Aircraft Engineer
Melvin Mallet

A well maintained plane can fly every day
for 30 years or more

Redundancy - Carry a Spare, Just in Case

An airliner is fundamentally different from a car. If things break down while flying you can't just pull over to the side of the road.

That's why the important parts of a plane are duplicated. There is *more than one* of each part, and not all are required.

This is called **redundancy**. There are extra parts, or systems, any one of which can fail and the plane will continue flying safely. A car has only one of everything. If any part of a car stops working, so will your car; this is not true of airliners.

EXAMPLES OF REDUNDANCY

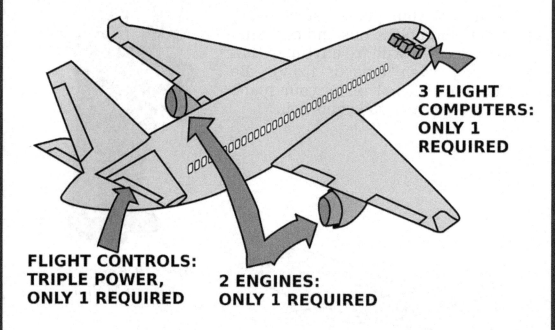

3 FLIGHT COMPUTERS: ONLY 1 REQUIRED

FLIGHT CONTROLS: TRIPLE POWER, ONLY 1 REQUIRED

2 ENGINES: ONLY 1 REQUIRED

Redundancy is like we are carrying spare parts, and those parts are already connected <u>and</u> operating.

Important lessons that aviators have learned: design it well, build it well, treat it well, and maintain it well. If we do these things your plane will look after you, always.

There simply are no better designed, manufactured or maintained machines. I love 'em!

Number One on the Fear List

After the Walkers had learned all they were going to learn about planes being safe I led them back to my Multimedia Presentation Room in the basement, and I thought about what to teach them next.

It occurred to me, seeing the tremendous progress they were making so far, that were ready for a big step. It was time for them to learn about the *scariest* part of flying!

But first, I think I'll have a little fun with them. They seem like good sports! I gave them each a piece of paper and a pencil.

"I'd like you to write down all of the things that freak you out about air travel. Don't be shy; this quiz is completely confidential and your names will not appear on the Internet or on TV."

While the family were completing their questionnaires I went to the back of the storeroom and rummaged around in a pile of boxes, preparing my highly sophisticated demonstration.

When I returned to the front of the room I asked the Walkers to fold their answer sheets and hand them to me. Placing the folded sheets on top of the slide projector I waddled to the back of the storeroom, returning with my demonstration apparatus: a box with a closed lid.

"Inside this box is the thing of which you are all afraid!"

Johnny raised his hand. "Felix, you haven't looked at our lists yet. How do you know what is on them?"

"I don't need to. Almost everyone who is afraid to fly is afraid of what is inside this box. Do you want to see it?"

The Walkers were nervous that the box would contain something gut-wrenchingly terrifying, but they were also curious.

I opened the box with a flourish, chiming "Ta-dah!" I held the box up for all to see.

"It is empty!" blurted a disappointed Jane.

Johnny, however, knew that just because you can't see something does not mean it is not real. "No, it isn't. The box is full of air."

"Very good, lad. Now who can guess what is on everybody's list?"

The Walkers stared the vacant stare of the perplexed.

"Let me give you a clue," I said as I shook the box violently: up-and-down; left-and-right; forwards and back.

The lights were on at Louise's house. "I know!" she said, "The answer is turbulence!"

"You betcha," I replied, "and you know what? Turbulence is just air! Let's look at some slides."

Lesson 10: Turbulence

Many people worry about turbulence. It may not be the number one thing on your freak-out list, but turbulence is so commonly mentioned that we thought that "bumpy air" deserved a lesson of its own.

So, let's start off with the best part first:

***As long as you take one
simple precaution,
turbulence can never harm you!***

We will talk about this precaution soon, but first consider this:

Your fear dragon might say...

"The wings will snap off, the plane will break into bits, or an 'air pocket' will make your plane fall from the sky."

None of this is true!

What is Turbulence?

Turbulence is simply *air that is not moving smoothly.*

Air is always moving around the planet. Sometimes it moves slowly and smoothly, like water in a lake. At other times it can be churned up, moving at different speeds and directions, like water going down the rapids.

When we fly through patches of this "bumpy air" we will feel ourselves being bumped up and down.

Bump Bump Bumpetty Bump

This is no problem, even though it feels bad. Your plane is VERY strong and is designed to handle this bumping.

There are many types of turbulence but all have one thing in common: whatever the cause, turbulence is just "bumpy air."

Let's talk about some of the causes of turbulence...

Gusty Winds

Sometimes the winds are **gusty**. You know what I mean: one minute the wind is howling, and the next minute it is calm. Then the wind starts blowing again, maybe from a different direction.

This is a common cause of turbulence.

GUSTY WINDS CAUSE BUMPY AIR!

This will make for a bumpy ride!

If your airline only flew when the winds were calm then you'd spend a lot of time waiting; it would often be quicker to ride a horse!

Instead, airliners have been designed to handle the bumps. Turbulence may feel uncomfortable, but it causes no problems. Some days will be bumpy, because of the wind.

Orographic Turbulence

When wind blows over or past something sticking up in the way, such as a mountain, it can get bumpy. Once your plane climbs above the mountains you can expect it to be smooth.

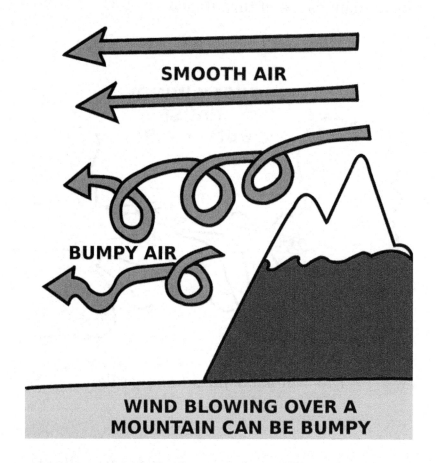

SMOOTH AIR

BUMPY AIR

WIND BLOWING OVER A MOUNTAIN CAN BE BUMPY

Orographic means: "to do with mountains."

Your pilots will avoid the worst of this turbulence by not flying too close to the mountains.

Some bumps may be unavoidable at low altitude, particularly if taking off from an airport surrounded by mountains. You can expect these bumps to reduce as you climb.

Convective Clouds

Some clouds look lumpy. The word "convective" means air is moving up and down inside a cloud; it is this air movement that gives these clouds their lumpy, "cauliflower" appearance.

**A BIG LUMPY CLOUD
CAN BE VERY BUMPY**

It is a good bet that such clouds are bumpy inside. Why not wait for a cloudless day to fly?—because sometimes you would have to wait for days!

Instead, airliners are built strong, and fitted with weather radar to help your pilots to see these clouds. Even at night, your pilots will fly around the biggest, but they cannot avoid them all. There may be a few bumps if it is cloudy.

Clear Air Turbulence

Sometimes the air is bumpy because wind moving at different speeds mixes together. If there are no clouds showing us where this bumpiness is occurring it is called *Clear Air Turbulence*. This kind of turbulence is difficult to detect.

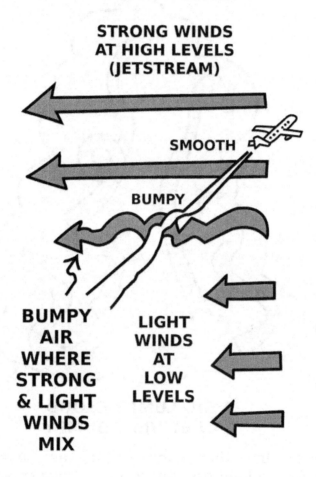

**STRONG WINDS
AT HIGH LEVELS
(JETSTREAM)**

SMOOTH

BUMPY

**BUMPY
AIR
WHERE
STRONG
& LIGHT
WINDS
MIX**

**LIGHT
WINDS
AT
LOW
LEVELS**

Even on the days when Clear Air Turbulence is likely your pilots may not know exactly when, or if, bumps will occur.

Sometimes it can get bumpy with little or no warning. This is no problem *if* you take an important safety precaution... we'll get to that shortly. Have you guessed what it is yet?

There are many reasons for turbulence but, whatever the cause:

> ***Turbulence is just bumpy air!***
> ***That's it, no big deal.***

There is a theory that coffee causes turbulence,
but the scientific data is inconclusive.

Why are the wings bouncing up and down?

You may notice, if you are seated near the wings, that they bounce up and down in turbulence.

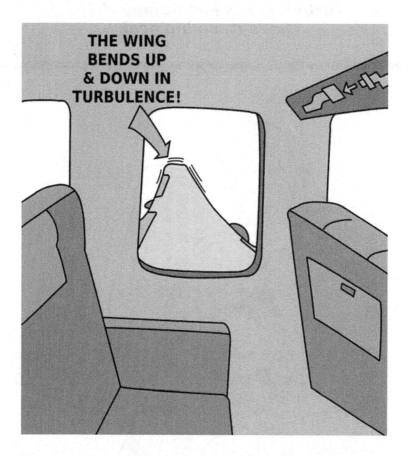

THE WING BENDS UP & DOWN IN TURBULENCE!

Don't freak out. They are supposed to do that!

One of the reasons why the wings are so unbelievably strong is that they are designed to have a bit of "give" in them. When the plane is bouncing along in turbulence you will see the wings bounce too.

It may look weird, but it is a *good thing*.

The people who designed your plane with flexible wings were absolute geniuses!

Seatbelts—the Number 1 Safety Precaution!

AN IMPORTANT SAFETY QUESTION:

Question: Is turbulence dangerous?

Answer: No *

* This is the fine print, the sneaky disclaimer that some companies use when they only want to tell you half of the story but have to put the rest in somewhere. So here it is: turbulence is not dangerous *if you wear your seatbelt*.

For those of you who don't like "fine print," here it is again:

Turbulence is not dangerous
IF YOU WEAR YOUR SEATBELT!

THE MOST IMPORTANT BIT OF SAFETY GEAR ON THE PLANE!

In the years since the Wright Brothers flew the first powered aeroplane we have learned some **important lessons:**

IMPORTANT LESSONS ABOUT TURBULENCE

1. If you wear your seatbelt you will **not** hit your head on the roof.

2. The wings will **not** fall off.

When the Seatbelt Sign is on you MUST have your seatbelt fastened!

When Should I Wear My Seatbelt?

Amelia says:

"ALWAYS wear your seatbelt when the seatbelt sign is on. It will be on for *takeoff* and *landing.*

"We will also turn it on if:

- We *know* it will be bumpy;

- We *think* it may be bumpy.

*First Officer
Amelia Airstart*

"You will hear a 'ding' when we turn it on, and usually an announcement. If the sign is on, wear your seatbelt!"

Sometimes your pilots will turn the seatbelt sign on even though the flight is smooth. This is done as a **precaution**.

Amelia also says,
"We'll turn the sign on because we think it *might* get bumpy, but it doesn't always turn out that way. Better safe than sorry!"

REMEMBER...
Your safety is our Number One concern.

If the seatbelt sign is turned on, **WEAR YOUR SEATBELT!**

When Else Should I Wear My Seatbelt?

Any time you are seated!

You should *always* have your seatbelt fastened when sitting in your seat, even if the seatbelt sign is off. You might not have it as tight as you would when the seatbelt sign is on, but you should at least have it on.

*This does not mean that you can't go to the toilet if the seatbelt sign is off. It just means that **when you are in your seat** you should have your seatbelt on. It's just common sense!*

Why? Because Your Pilots Cannot Avoid All Turbulence!

Air is continually in motion around the Earth, and it is simply not possible to avoid all turbulence.

Your pilots can avoid the worst *convective* turbulence by flying around the biggest clouds. Even at night, their weather radar shows them the location of those clouds.

However, they can't avoid *all* clouds. Some days there are lots of clouds in the sky..

There are other kinds of turbulence too, difficult to detect, which can result in unexpected bumps.

It is plain old common sense: wear your seatbelt any time you are seated!

Aviation Safety IQ Test

To remain perfectly safe in turbulence:
  A) Stick yourself to the seat with glue
  B) Strap pillows to your entire body
  C) Wear your seatbelt

Answer: C, of course! Did you really have to check?

Queasy Guts

I switched off the projector. "Are there any
questions about turbulence? It really is just bumpy air and, in the
right frame of mind, can be considered good fun."

Louise frowned. "Sometimes I feel queasy in turbulence. How can
that be good fun?"

"Well, okay. I can see how you might not enjoy that. But there are
preparations you can do to lessen any queasiness you might feel.
There are some medications that can help, but you should ask your
doctor for advice about this to see if they are right for you."

"Are there natural ways I can reduce motion sickness?"

"Sure! There are lots of dietary ideas you can consider. For
example, you might avoid dairy foods or very salty foods before flying,

and you should make sure you are well hydrated.

Larry looked up, as if I'd made some great revelation, and smiled. "I always drink before I fly!"

I growled. I knew that he was talking about one of the greatest misconceptions that adults have — alcohol. That applies doubly to people trying to deal with fear.

"I'm not talking about booze, Larry. That will not help. When you fly you want to be in control of yourself, your body and your emotions. I think we all know what happens when *you* drink alcohol."

The rest of the family chuckled as Larry's face reddened — he knew exactly the incident in his past I was talking about.

I continued, returning to the topic of queasiness. "You could also consider trying to get a window or an aisle seat. Looking into the distance can help, rather than having your head buried in a book. There are plenty of other things you can try, and you probably have a few good ideas of your own. Do some research and don't let it beat you. The more you overcome motion sickness, the less it will affect you. This is called 'desensitisation'."

I have to confess, I was feeling a little green after this conversation, so I changed the subject. "I've been going through the lists that you made about things that freak you out when you fly. Well done... they are *very* comprehensive.

"It can be helpful to realise that you are not alone in your fears; there are many people afraid of exactly the same things as you."

Except... I raised an eyebrow and looked at Larry, who reddened further. "Except for *you* Larry. This fear on your list is very unusual."

"Hey! I thought you said the quiz was confidential!" said Larry, defensively.

"Okay, okay. We'll keep that one between us," I said, chuckling. "Your confidentiality is assured!"

I held the lists in front of my face and demonstrated Doc Leroy's deep breathing technique, dragon-style. *In... one... two... three... Out...*

"I'm sure you know, by now, that Fear Dragons work on many levels. Sometimes we do big fear, like my TV news work. Other times we work on a one-on-one basis with your own individual fears. These individual fears can be just as effective.

"In fact, I want to show some special things that freak people out about flying. Maybe when we talk about these things, even if they are not on *your* personal fear list, you will not feel so alone."

The Walkers settled back in their seats and I restarted the projector. It was time to show them some first-class *freakouts.*

Felix's Most Unusual
FEAR OF FLYING COURSE
SLIDE PRESENTATION

Lesson 11: F-F-Freakouts!

Unusual events and circumstances can easily be used for mischief by a fertile imagination.

When combined with past experiences that you did not completely understand and a smattering of incomplete knowledge, *freakout events* can give your dragon all the food it needs!

Most of the time flying is completely uneventful and routine. Sometimes, however, unusual things do happen. We'll talk about some of them. It is important to know that *all* of these events are:

- considered in advance;
- prepared for; and
- handled safely.

You will see that they are nothing to be concerned about.

Sometimes people have other fears, not related to flying, which become their main "freakout." We'll talk about some of those too.

Remember, as unusual as a situation or event may seem:

> ***Pilots and flight attendants fly up to 500 flights every year and nothing happens to them.***

Is this you?

Some people just won't take "It's Okay" for an answer.

Claustrophobia

Some people don't like flying because they have a fear of being trapped in an enclosed space. This fear is called *claustrophobia*.

People who have this fear might have problems entering an elevator, or being in a small room.

Rather than being a fear of flying, claustrophobia has its roots elsewhere; some professional counselling may assist.

Some people find that dealing with their fear of flying helps them to deal with their claustrophobia, because the two can be related.

Fear of Heights

Sometimes people with a fear of heights transfer this into a fear of flying.

This kind of makes sense as planes *do* fly high in the sky, but flying in a plane is different.

You are securely seated inside a multi-million dollar machine that has been specifically designed to be safe.

YOUR SEAT IS A MULTI-MILLION DOLLAR FULLY ENCLOSED SAFETY HARNESS!

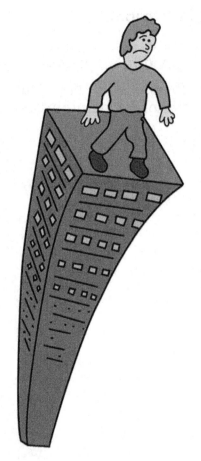

Relax: You Cannot Fall!

Even some airline crewmembers are afraid of heights but they have *no problem* flying an aeroplane; they know that planes are different from other heights... you cannot fall!

Engineering Delays

Occasionally a flight will be delayed for a mechanical reason. The engineers may need extra time to fix your aircraft prior to departure, which means that your flight will depart late.

Sometimes this delay occurs before you get on board. Your waiting time is spent in the terminal; you will have the luxury of walking around and listening to other passengers complaining.

At other times, however, the problem is not revealed until your pilots are well into their pre-flight checks. You may have already boarded the aircraft. This is not so much fun.

***Some people let a delay announcement
fuel their fear dragon.***

Should I be concerned if the airplane needs fixing? No, because we *are* fixing it!

All machines need maintenance. Look after them well and machines will last for decades.

Engineer Mel says:

"We want our airliners to last a long time, flying safely every time. That's why we check them before *every* flight, and deal with any problem that we find.

"Some passengers get cranky about the extra time this takes. Nobody likes to be delayed, but getting cranky about it is nuts!"

Aircraft Engineer
Melvin Mallet

Remember, we are doing <u>exactly</u> what you want us to do... taking care of SAFETY before anything else.

You can expect to be told about the cause and likely duration of a lengthy delay. Some fearful flyers allow the dragon in their mind to use this information to imagine carnage, catastrophe and chaos. There is no need for this kind of thinking. Instead, try this:

<u>Relax and Trust.</u>
There is NO WAY that your plane is going ANYWHERE until your highly qualified pilots and engineers are 100% sure that it is safe.

And shut that dragon up... it is upsetting the other passengers!

The Half-Way Yuckies

On a long flight you may find, after the excitement of departure and the meal service, that there can be a difficult time.

In the middle of the night, when the other passengers are asleep, your imagination may be wide awake.

This is a perfect time, with no other distractions, for your imagination to amuse you. You might start thinking "37,000 feet is *really* high," or all sorts of other disturbing thoughts. With the other passengers asleep, you may feel truly alone—just you and your dragon.

So here's the news:

Nothing is wrong.

All is as it should be.

If it wasn't you <u>would</u> be told.

Keep busy! Some ideas to help fight the half-way yuckies:

1. If you have the luxury of an in-flight entertainment system, watch a movie. This works best if it is a great movie that you have been looking forward to seeing.

   TIP: On a long flight with an on-demand movie system save the movie you REALLY want to see for later. Watch your second choice first and save the great movie for later, when you know you will need distraction.

2. Read a book or do a crossword, sudoku or other tricky puzzles. Do not worry about waking others up with your reading light... you paid for the ticket and the electricity; use it if you wish. They will sleep anyway if they are tired enough.

3. Listen to some music, comedy or discussion on the inflight entertainment system. Perhaps you have some stuff stored on your personal audio/video player—the more interesting the better!

4. Get up and go for a walk (only if the flight is smooth and the seatbelt sign is off, of course). Go to the toilet. Find a flight attendant and ask for a drink of water, and perhaps have a chat.

   The *half-way yuckies* occur on a long flight because the quiet time, when nothing else is going on, is a playground for your imagination. If you can keep you mind busy with other things then your imagination will be less likely to drift off to places you'd rather it didn't.

HALF-WAY YUCKIES COMBAT PLAN
Plan ahead some brain activities that you *know* you are going to enjoy... a great book, crosswords, music, podcasts, videos, etc.

Worry? I'm far too busy for that!

Go-Arounds

Sometimes, if the conditions for landing are not perfect, your pilots will apply full power and climb away instead of landing. This is called a "go-around."

There are a range of reasons they might do this and all of them are *nothing to worry about.*

Reasons for a go-around include:

- Unusual wind gusts
- Runway still occupied by another aircraft
- Fog or low cloud obscuring the runway
- Ducks crossing the runway

None of these present a problem. Your pilots will simply fly around and have another go.

If the reason for the go-around was bad weather then they may have to fly to another airport with better weather, or fly around waiting for the weather to improve. Whichever option they choose, they always make sure that there is plenty of fuel.

IN A GO-AROUND YOU WILL HEAR AND FEEL...

1. **Hear** the engine noise increase as the engines go to full power.

2. **Feel** the aircraft point "upwards" as you start climbing away from the ground.

3. **Feel** yourself pushed back in your seat, as a combination of the aircraft pointing upwards and accelerating.

4. **Hear** the "Whir-Clu-Clunk" when the wheels are retracted (raised).

It may be a while before an announcement is made telling you what happened because your pilots will be busy preparing for the next approach and landing. Don't let this delay in talking to you feed your dragon—just because the pilots have not yet told you what happened does not mean that you should be concerned.

A go-around is not an everyday occurrence, but does happen from time to time. It is an important part of airline safety.

Pilots are taught from their very first lesson:

> *If a landing doesn't look perfect,*
> *go-around and have another go!*

Don't freak out about go-arounds. They are a **good thing!**

Engine Failure

For modern aircraft, an *engine failure* is a very rare event. Reasons for an engine to stop working correctly include mechanical failure and "bird strike."

Airliners have more than one engine and pilots are well trained, so an engine failure is *not* a catastrophe. It is simply *inconvenient,* because the pilots may decide to land at a nearby airport as a precaution.

The *News* may make a big hullabaloo about an engine failure, but it is not a big deal at all — except for the bird!

What If All The Engines Fail?

If all the engines fail your plane will NOT
                                            FALL
                                            FROM
                                            THE
                                            SKY!

...Instead, it will   G
                               L
                                   I
                                        D
                                            E   beautifully!

In "A Very Dangerous Experiment" (Lesson 8) we saw that *lift*, the force which holds your plane up, is created by the wings.

The engines do not create lift; rather, the engines maintain our speed through the air by overcoming the *drag* force.

Another way of maintaining our speed through the air is to gradually descend. This requires no engine power, and is called *gliding*.

In fact, a normal descent in an airliner is a glide-descent. The engines are reduced to minimum power and airspeed is maintained by descending. From cruise altitude your aircraft can glide for about 240 kilometres (150 miles), taking about 20 minutes to come down (just like a normal descent to your destination). Plenty of time to get at least one engine started again or plan where to land.

All aeroplanes are natural gliders.

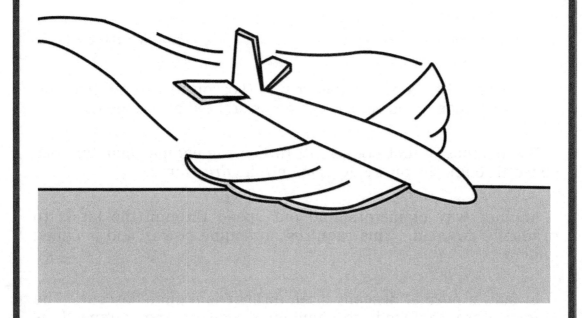

Air Pockets

Everyone has heard someone say "I hate those air pockets!"

They even talk about air pockets on the "news" shows. You would be forgiven for thinking that an air pocket is a hole in the sky, with no air in it, into which your airliner will fall.

The news people like using the word "plummet" in such stories. You are being deceived by them.

In fact:

There is *<u>no such thing</u>* *as an air pocket!*

"Air pockets" are a completely made up concept, nothing more than turbulence; we talked about turbulence in the previous section.

Your aeroplane has *no problem* with turbulence and neither will you *if you wear your seatbelt!*

Two air pockets... *time to go home.*

Numbers

Louise, like all of the Walkers, was learning some great stuff about flying but still she was unhappy. She was one of those people who felt that, no matter how small the chance, if something bad was going to happen it would happen to her.

I figured we needed to talk about numbers. Humans have very little understanding of numbers and what they really mean. They are driven by what they "feel" is right, even if the numbers prove that reality is quite different.

"Have you ever bought a lottery ticket Louise?"

"Sure, occasionally I buy a ticket."

"What are the odds of winning?"

Louise shrugged. "One in a million. One in ten million. I don't know exactly."

"And have you ever won the first prize in a lottery?"

"Well, no. It is not very likely."

And yet she keeps buying tickets! "Louise, what would you do if you won the lottery?"

Her eyes lit up. "Oh, I've thought all about that. I'd pay off our house, we'd go on a nice holiday, maybe get a boat. I'd have lots of new shoes, and I might even get a boob job."

I dug a little deeper. "So, you've thought about it. Why? It really isn't very likely that you will win. You said yourself the odds are millions to one against."

Dreamily, she replied, "Yes, but it is fun to imagine."

"Has it occurred to you that you do exactly the same thing with flying? The odds of something bad happening to you on an airliner are millions to one against, yet you allow your imagination to come up with all kinds of horrible stories."

Louise frowned at the comparison. "That's different. The consequences are far worse with an airliner."

"Maybe, but the numbers are similar. The chances of being killed on an airline flight are millions to one against. The exact figures change, from year to year, and depend somewhat upon where in the world you are flying. Statistics are tricky things, but I can give you an example...

"Let's say your chances of dying on an airline flight are, on average, about 1 in 3 million. That's globally, including all of the tinpot airlines too. If you just look at the top safety airlines that goes up to, say, 1 in 9 million. For argument's sake, let's assume it is about 1 in 5 million in a country with a good safety record."

"So what? One in five million? It could still happen," asked Louise.

"Sure, but does anyone here really know how big these numbers are? Does anyone really know how big a number a million is?"

Johnny piped up, "I do Felix. A million dollars is what a millionaire has one of."

"Very good Johnny, but a millionaire does not carry around his money in one dollar notes or coins. He has a few one-hundred dollar bills in his pocket for emergencies, and puts the rest in the bank or into some investment. He never actually sees the money. He has no better idea about *one million* than you."

"Do *you* know what these numbers mean?" asked Louise.

"Actually, yes. Let's go for a walk."

I led my curious students out of the presentation room, down the hallway, and into the lift. I pressed the button labelled *Swimming Pool* and Johnny got excited.

"Wow! Are we going for a swim Felix?"

"Oh no, we don't use the pool for swimming. Dragons don't particularly like water. Here we are," I said as the lift arrived at the pool level.

I invited them in. "Welcome to the Fear of Numbers Department!"

As they entered, Larry noticed that the pool was filled with yellow.

"That is disgusting. They really should keep kids out of it." As he got closer to the pool, however, he realised that the pool was not filled with yellow water at all. It was, in fact, filled with tennis balls.

The pool room was huge. Complete with grandstand seating for several hundred dragons, it was home to an Olympic size swimming pool. It would have been the perfect venue for a major swimming carnival, except for the lack of water.

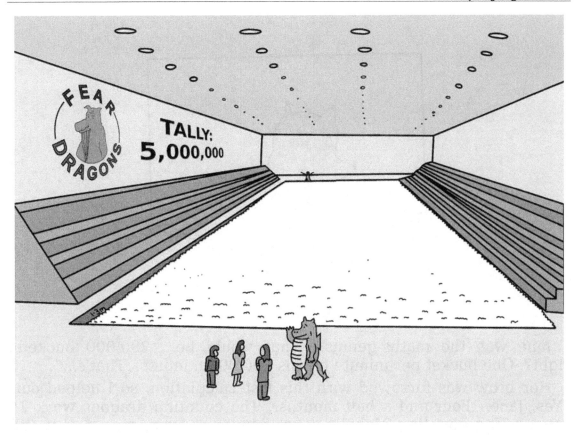

I sent Larry way down the other end of the pool, so that the others could truly appreciate its size. They could hardly see him; the pool was immense.

"What is this room for?" asked Louise.

"Well, our Fear of Numbers dragons use it for counting practice. They tell me there are exactly 5 million tennis balls in that pool."

"Five million. Wow. It must be a big job to count them," said Larry.

"It sure is. They have teams of dragons working day and night, carrying buckets of balls from this pool to our other pool down the hall. They count balls into buckets, and count the number of buckets they move. Can you guess how long it takes?"

Louise wanted the details. "How big are the buckets?"

"Well, each bucket holds 25 tennis balls, and they manage to count and move one bucketful every minute."

Jane was the maths-genius: "That would be... 200,000 buckets, right? One bucket per minute means 200,000 minutes. That's..."

Her brow was furrowed with this last calculation, so I helped out: "Yes, Jane. Four and a half months. The counting dragons work 24 hours a day, counting 25 balls every minute of every day, and it still takes them four and a half months to count the lot."

Larry asked, "What happens if they lose count?"

"That really bugs them. Actually, sometimes I'll sneak in here and throw an extra ball into the pool, just to mess up their count. They hate it when I do that, because they have to start again!"

Johnny chuckled, imagining the look on the counting dragon's faces when, after shifting 200,000 buckets of balls, they realise they have one ball left over. Priceless!

I smiled too. "Actually, I added an extra ball yesterday, but I made a mistake. It turns out that the ball I added to the pool was a gift from my granma and has my name written on it. If the counting dragons find it they will know about my little game and I will be in big trouble. Perhaps you could help me find *that* ball."

The Walkers agreed to help me find my missing tennis ball. Louise asked, "Which part of the pool did you put it in?"

I waved vaguely at the pool. "I tossed it in over there, but unfortunately the balls are stirred up and mixed every night. It could be anywhere now. It could be on the surface, or four feet deep, or somewhere in between. It could be near the edge, or right out in the middle, or anywhere else."

So my helpful students started searching for that one particular ball. Johnny searched out in the middle of the pool, and Jane ran down to the far end and look there. Louise searched the area near where I had thrown the ball in, and Larry reached deep below the surface pulling balls out and inspecting them.

After about half an hour of searching the Walkers were ready to give up. Of course, they had not found the ball, nor did I expect them to. There were just too many balls in the pool.

Louise said, "We will never find that ball Felix. It is impossible!"
I grinned. "No Louise. Just very, very unlikely."

ADVERTISEMENT

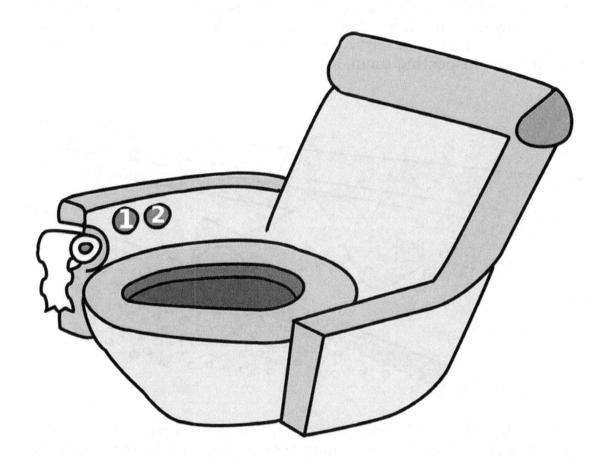

**The New
Enhanced Economy Seat**

specially designed for nervous flyers.

PART THREE

Fly With Me

Noises Make Pictures

"I want to tell you a little more about how we work at Fear Dragons, so that you will better understand how fears are made."

I had the Walkers' attention... who wouldn't want to know such things? "Let's talk about dentists," I said as I put up an image on the screen.

"You know and I know that dentists are good people and there is nothing to be afraid about at the dentist. They are there to help with your dental health and wellbeing. However, I got this photo from the *Fear of Dentists* department, to show you how we can twist the truth to make you afraid."

Larry squirmed in his seat and asked, "Why are you showing us this? I thought we were here to talk about fear of flying."

"Quite so, but I do have a reason," I said as I walked to the back of the storeroom and retrieved a music player from a shelf above the vat of jellyfish.

Setting up the player, I explained. "I have a recording of an unusual sound and I want you to close your eyes and listen. Then I want you to tell me what it is. Are you ready?"

The whole family nodded in agreement. They closed their eyes and listened:

BZZZTZZZ ZZTZ

SLURP! GURGLE!

The sound that I played was a high pitched whine, interspersed with occasional liquidy sounds as the pitch lowered slightly. The Walkers, young and old, knew exactly what that sound was, all having spent time in the dentist's chair.

Afterwards I asked, "So what did you hear?"

Johnny replied first. "That was the dentist man drilling a tooth!"

"Yes, that's it," said Jane. "And it sounded like the drill sprayed mouth juice all over the place, and then the patient gargled the spit-water."

"What do you think, Louise?"

"I would have to agree. We've got a great dentist and I don't mind going there, but the sound of the drill is not particularly pleasant."

Larry, who had never been a big fan of visiting the dentist, made his view perfectly clear: "I'd rather not talk about it. I want the gas."

These were exactly the kind of comments I had expected. They were completely wrong, but I didn't tell them that yet. Instead I asked, "Why do you think it was a dentist's drill?"

"It is obvious," said Larry. "You showed us a picture of a dentist."

"Yes, but I didn't say that the sound and the image were related. I showed you an image of a dentist to set the scene, to get your mind into a certain way of thinking."

"Are you saying that it *wasn't* a dentist's drill?" asked Louise.

"All I'm saying is that because you were predisposed to expecting something you were ready to jump to a conclusion when you heard the sound."

Jane knew what I was talking about. "Artistry of the mind!"

"Very good Jane! You go to the top of the class!" I was impressed by her leap of understanding. Jane beamed.

"Er, what are you both talking about?" asked Larry.

"First, I pre-programmed your mind by getting you thinking about dentists. Then, when I played you the sound, your imagination grabbed it and used it. You matched the sound to your preconceived ideas and your mind invented the rest. The simplest explanation to make the story complete was a dentist's drill."

Larry looked confused. "What does that have to do with Fear of Flying? We are not afraid of dentists. If we were we'd have signed up for a *Fear of Dentists* course!"

I spelled it out: "You do this kind of thing when you fly on a plane!"

Three of the Walkers still looked puzzled, but Jane provided the explanation. "Felix is saying that because we are afraid of flying we are already expecting some kind of disaster to occur. Then, when we hear a strange sound, we naturally imagine the worst!"

Louise grinned, getting it at last. "It is amazing how easily our minds were led down the wrong path with the dentist! So what *was* the sound you played us? Was it something dangerous or scary?"

Rather than reply, I showed a photo of myself mixing a drink using a blender, and then played the sound clip again.

This time the same sounds that had made the Walkers think about dentists sounded like me using a blender then gargling a drink.

"Was it something dangerous? Yes, but only because of the ingredients!"

Felix's Most Unusual
FEAR OF FLYING COURSE
SLIDE PRESENTATION

Lesson 12: What's That Noise?

First Officer Bernoulli

You *will* hear some strange noises when you fly.

Sometimes, because you don't know what they are, the everyday sounds of flight can be magnified by your mind into portents of doom. The dragon in your mind loves this kind of stuff.

The cure, of course, is knowledge.

Join us for a short flight so that we can talk about some of these noises. You will see that they are a normal part of flying and are nothing to be worried about.

I will now make an announcement over the aircraft's public address system. Please pay attention, in case I say something important...

"Thanks for joining us. We have a planned flight time of 50 minutes, and expect smooth flying conditions. You may hear some sounds which disturb you. Don't worry... all is well!"

Remember:
just because _you_ don't know what a noise is
does not mean that there is a problem.

The first strange sound occurs as we taxi out...

Before Takeoff: "Donk....Donk......Donk"

When your plane is taxiing (which means driving around on the ground), you may hear an occasional "donk" sound. We just ran over something!

The **taxiways**, which are the roads we drive on to get to the runway, have lights in the middle. This is so we can find our way during the night.

Each light has a protective metal cover. The light and its cover sticks up out of the ground so that the light can be seen from a long distance. They are designed to be run over.

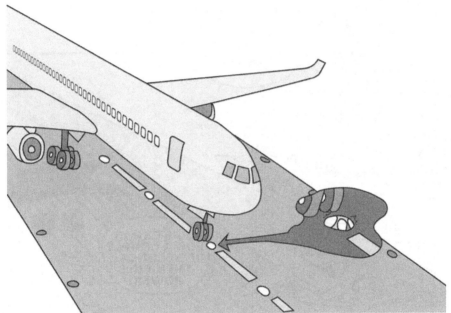

The lights that mark the centre of the taxiway make "donk" sounds as we drive over them.

There is a bump as we drive over these lights, and it is perfectly normal to run over a few. You might even hear a "donk" or two during the takeoff; lights mark the centre of the runway too!

The next strange sound occurs at takeoff...

Takeoff: "Quiet Roar, then Loud Roar"

Jet engines are fabulous things; they produce *lots* of power and we love them.

When we line up on the runway and get our *take-off clearance* from the control tower you'll hear the engines get louder.

We set the engines to MEDIUM power for a few seconds to check that everything is working properly. Then we apply FULL POWER.

That is why you will hear the engines get louder, and then get louder again as we "give 'em the juice."

In very cold weather, especially if it has been snowing or raining, we may run the engines for longer at medium power before applying full power. This is normal.

The next strange sound occurs after take-off...

After Takeoff: "Whir Clu-Clunk!"

Immediately after take-off we **retract the landing gear**. That's pilot talk for raising the wheels.

The machinery that lifts the wheels into their compartments and closes the doors that cover them makes some noise.

We need the wheels hanging out for take-off and landing, but they get hidden away behind doors when we are in the air so that they do not cause *drag*.

Drag would slow us down and make us need more fuel to get to our destination. More fuel means we'd need to charge you more for your plane ticket. The "whir-clu-clunk" is a good sound that saves you money!

The next strange sound can sometimes occur during climb...

Climb: "Engines Quiet, We are Descending!"

No we are not. This is an illusion! Sometimes after taking off from a busy airport we have to **level-off** during the climb because there is another plane flying above us. Air Traffic Control makes sure there is plenty of space between our planes, but they might ask us to fly level until the other aircraft passes.

You may find this disturbing because, all of a sudden, the engines go quiet and it *feels* like we are descending.

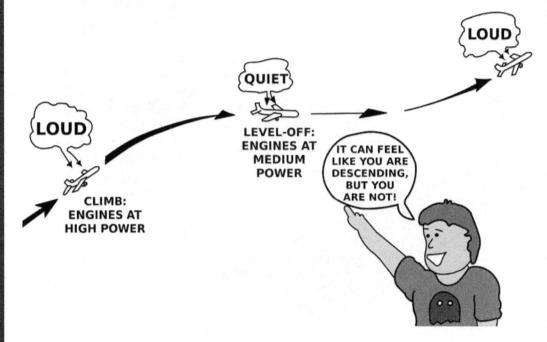

You get used to the loud noise of the engines at full power. Therefore, when we reduce them to <u>medium</u> power for level flight it can seem very quiet. Don't worry, the engines are doing exactly the amount of work needed to fly level!

Because you *were* going up but *now* you are flying level, it *feels* like you are going down. **You are not.**

The next strange sound can occur during the descent...

Start of Descent: "We're going Down!"

Eventually we need to **descend** (that's pilot talk for "go down") so that we can land at our destination.

You've been listening to the engines at medium power for quite a while now, so when we reduce engine power for our descent it can seem very quiet. This is normal.

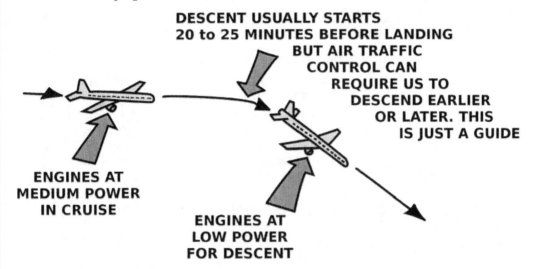

DESCENT USUALLY STARTS 20 to 25 MINUTES BEFORE LANDING BUT AIR TRAFFIC CONTROL CAN REQUIRE US TO DESCEND EARLIER OR LATER. THIS IS JUST A GUIDE

ENGINES AT MEDIUM POWER IN CRUISE

ENGINES AT LOW POWER FOR DESCENT

DESCENT MAY SEEM VERY QUIET BECAUSE YOU ARE USED TO LISTENING TO THE ENGINES AT MEDIUM POWER. THIS IS NORMAL!

We start our descent about 240 kilometres (150 miles) out, depending upon: how high we are, the wind direction, and wind speed.

The next strange sound sometimes occurs during descent...

Descent: "Speedbrake Rumble"

Sometimes during the descent you might hear, or feel, a slight rumble for a short period. This is caused by our speedbrake.

The speedbrake is a small set of flaps that pop up on top of each wing. You would see this if you had a window seat near the wing. The speedbrake reduces the lift produced by the wing and creates extra drag, allowing us to descend or decelerate more quickly. A side-effect is some rumbling vibration. This is perfectly normal.

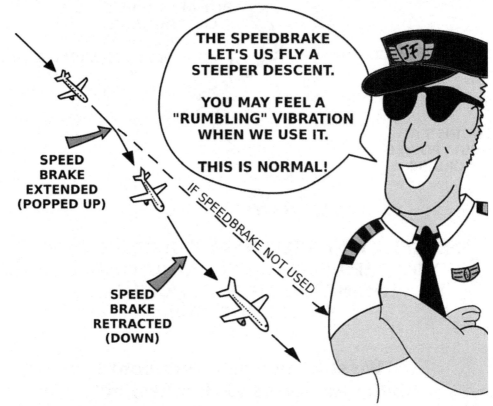

SPEED BRAKE EXTENDED (POPPED UP)

THE SPEEDBRAKE LET'S US FLY A STEEPER DESCENT.

YOU MAY FEEL A "RUMBLING" VIBRATION WHEN WE USE IT.

THIS IS NORMAL!

IF SPEEDBRAKE NOT USED

SPEED BRAKE RETRACTED (DOWN)

The speedbrake helps us fly a steeper descent path, something we may need to do if the wind is blowing us toward the destination airport during our descent. If we did nothing we'd be TOO HIGH when we get there. So, we make the rumble.

The next sound you may hear is that "whir-clu-clunk" again...

Gear Down: "Whir Clu-Clunk!"

You guessed it... we are getting close to landing so it is time to put the wheels down.

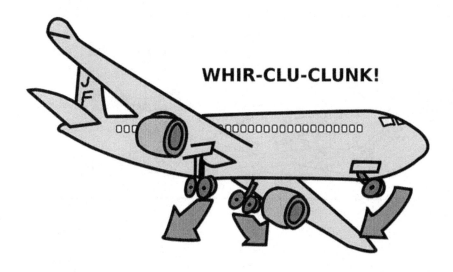

WHIR-CLU-CLUNK!

"Dangle the Dunlops!"

In pilot talk, this is called **extending the landing gear.**

Just like when we raised the wheels after take off, lowering the wheels makes a strange noise as the doors open and the wheels lock down into position. It is perfectly normal.

What goes up, must come down!

Sometimes, if the air is bumpy, you might hear another sound...

Approach: "Engines Loud, Quiet, Loud..."

Some days the air is windy and gusty. This means that the air is bumpy and moving at different speeds in different places.

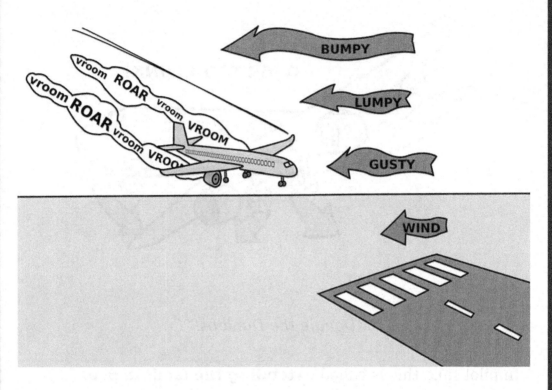

To keep our speed through the air constant we need to increase and decrease power from the engines. We will make power adjustments all the way through the **approach**, and you will hear the engine sounds change as we do this.

This is perfectly normal (and kinda fun, actually!)

Approach *is what pilots call the last part of the flight when we are "approaching" the runway.*

After we land another sound may take you by surprise...

After Landing: "Reverse Thrust ROAAR!"

After we touch down we will usually use **reverse thrust** to help slow the plane down.

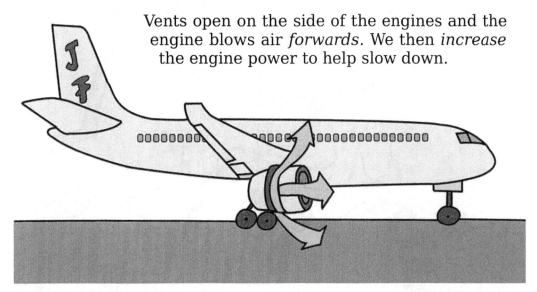

Vents open on the side of the engines and the engine blows air *forwards*. We then *increase* the engine power to help slow down.

You will definitely hear a loud roar if we use reverse thrust and, of course, this is another perfectly normal sound.

We've talked about a few of the noises you'll hear when you fly. There are others too, also perfectly normal.

If you are unsure about any sound you hear—ask someone! Ask your flight attendant, or perhaps the person sitting next to you, if she is a regular flyer. There is no reason to let your imagination run amok.

Bernoulli

Thanks for joining us for this short flight. It has been a pleasure having you aboard!

Puppetry

"We have talked about many ways in which your fears can be brought to life. From turbulence to weird noises, from air pockets to terrorists, there are many ways in which I can pull your strings."

I put up a picture which showed a person being controlled like a puppet, with a dragon as the puppeteer.

"Do you think this image represents the truth?"

"Well," said Jane, "It kind of *seems* true. I do sometimes feel that fear is controlling my life."

"Very good, Jane. The best lies *do* have an air of truth about them. It helps them get past your normal defences so that they can lodge in your mind and become beliefs."

Larry and Louise thought about this. They had indeed come to realise that many of their beliefs were built on misunderstandings, half-truths and lies. It was not hard to imagine a fear dragon using fear to control their every move, just as if they were puppets on a stage.

"Let me ask you another question. If you were to cut the strings of a puppet, what would happen?"

"The puppet would fall to the ground, silly!" said Johnny.

"Right! But what if you cut your own strings of fear? A puppeteer can't control you without the strings attached, but would you actually fall to the ground?"

To emphasise my point I held a large pair of scissors up in the air. I opened and closed them, the click of the shears cutting imaginary strings.

"No," said Larry. "In fact, I'd probably walk taller without the burden of fear."

"Give that man a hotdog! You are right Larry. The image that I showed you, of me being a puppeteer and controlling your life is, in large part, a lie. It kind of feels like the truth but, in fact, is designed to make you feel helpless—a plaything subject to *my* every whim and fancy. We know that this is not true.

"You can, of course, stand without my help. You can be in control of your life. You just have to make the choice to cut the strings of fear!"

"How can I cut strings I can't even see?" asked Louise.

"You can feel them, Louise, when you are tense, or anxious, or afraid. Even when your tornado spins full cycle and you are in the grip of panic, you can feel the strings of fear."

"But how do we cut those strings?" asked Jane.

"There are many ways, but all depend on being aware that fear is controlling you. When you sense this, try visualising a pair of scissors. Make an imaginary pair of scissors with your fingers, if you like, and pretend to cut them."

"Do these visualisation methods work?" asked Larry.

"Why not give it a go? All of you, stand up here at the front of the class and imagine you are puppets. Dance around like you are being controlled by a puppeteer. That is what it is like to have your life ruled by fear."

"I feel stupid," said Larry, strutting around like a Thunderbird.

"Good. You look stupid. But you can do something about it. Now I want you to make finger-scissors and cut the imaginary strings that are controlling you."

The Walkers cut their strings and no one fell to the ground. I was very proud of them.

"Any time you take a positive action and do not let fear rule your life you cut a puppeteer's string. *You* are in control of your life and do not need the support of a fear dragon. *You* are in control and fear is not your master."

Felix's Most Unusual
FEAR OF FLYING COURSE
SLIDE PRESENTATION

Lesson 13: <u>You</u> Are In Control

A common part of some people's fear of flying is concern that they are *not in control.*

Perhaps you feel, when you are sitting in an airliner, that you have no control over your fate.

For example, you may feel that you have no control because:

- The plane is flown by others (pilots)
- You are fed by others (flight attendants)
- The plane is fixed by others (engineers)
- The plane is managed by others (air traffic controllers)

It may be that you don't really understand what those people are doing, and no one seems to have the time to explain.

RELAX
All of these people are doing their jobs *for you,* and have spent their entire careers learning to do their jobs well.

Let <u>them</u> control the plane.
They are better at it than you!
(just as you are better at what you do than they would be)

There are, however, many things about flying and your safety that you *do* have control over. You are not just "cargo." If you want to take a more active role then you simply have to decide to get involved.

This lesson discusses some ways in which you can be more *in control* and participate more fully in your flight experience.

Step one is to keep that stupid dragon on a leash! You know more about flying now than you did before this course; use this information to keep your imagination in check!

Lets talk about some ideas to put you back in the driver's seat when you fly...

Relax!

Easier said than done? Impossible? *Anyone* can take steps to make themselves more relaxed. We discussed some relaxation techniques in Lesson 4.

Here is another variation of a deep breathing technique which, like the other techniques, shows that your mind and body are closely related.

Deep Breathing Exercise 3

Pick a part of your body and tense all of the muscles in that part of your body. For example, start with your feet.

When you have tensed those muscles, slowly breathe in. Count to three as you inhale. Then, hold your breathe for another slow count of three.

As you slowly exhale, say the word *"relax"* and completely relax the tension in your muscles.

MUSCLE TENSION AND RELAXATION

1. Tense a muscle group;
2. Inhale, deeply and slowly;
3. Hold your breathe for a count of three;
4. Exhale, saying RELAX, relaxing those muscles as you do.
5. Repeat, again for those muscles if required, or moving on to a different muscle group.

You may realise, as you relax the tension on each muscle group, that you were surprisingly tense. When you deliberately release all muscle tension with this exercise you will relax your body. This, in turn, relaxes your mind.

You can try this exercise quickly, targeting muscles that you know are tense, or you can take your time and apply it to your whole body a bit at a time. For example, start with your feet, move up through your legs, abdomen, chest, arms, hands, neck, face, etc..

As we said earlier, there are many relaxation techniques that can help, and some experimentation is useful. The nice thing about this particular technique is that your body will associate relaxation with the word *"relax,"* giving that word more power to help you do just that.

With practice, relaxation can be as simple as saying the word *relax!*

Get to the Airport Early!

You may not like airports and are probably not looking forward to your flight. You may, therefore, delay going to the airport until the last minute.

If you end up running late, however, your anxiety will be worse. Concern about missing your flight, luggage juggling and check-in queues will be followed by a mad dash for the departure gate. After discovering that it is at the far end of the terminal and they are calling "final boarding," you will *not* be relaxed.

That is *no way* to start a flight. By the time you sit down on the aircraft your nerves will be fried and your batteries drained.

Aim to be as relaxed as you can when you get on-board. Getting to the airport early helps to "save your batteries" for when you really need them.

Arrive at the airport early and let everyone else run around like a bunch of mad chickens

Before You Fly

By arriving early you will be more relaxed and will have time for other tasks that put you *in control* of your situation.

1. **Request the seat you want**
   If you are early you will have the pick of the seats, if the airline you have chosen has assigned seating. Some nervous flyers prefer a window seat, some prefer an aisle seat. Maybe requesting a seat toward the front of the cabin will suit you more.

   Don't worry, however, if you don't get the exact seat you want. They are all good and all will arrive at your destination at about the same time!

   NOTE: Some airlines allow check-in and seat allocation over the Internet, possibly with an extra fee for this privilege. Find out your airline's policy when you buy the ticket, including the earliest time you can log in with your request —first in, best dressed! If where you sit is important, understanding how and when seats are assigned is a <u>good thing</u> for you.

2. **Get Some Activities**
   To avoid giving your imagination too much spare time, make sure you have some things keep your mind occupied: books, puzzles, postcards, snacks etc.

3. **Use the airport toilet before you board**
   A common sense idea which gives you one less thing to worry about. *There is nothing wrong with aircraft toilets, but there can be a wait involved (particularly after meals when everyone seems to get the same great idea).*

Listen To The Safety Demonstration Carefully

As your plane leaves the terminal, taxiing towards the runway for takeoff, your flight attendants will do an exotic performance called the "Safety Demonstration."

DO NOT freakout thinking that they are talking about crashing. They are simply telling you about some of the excellent safety equipment on-board, and some of the things that have been learned about being safe. THEY ARE *NOT* SAYING THAT YOU ARE GOING TO CRASH!

The Safety Demonstration will include:

- How to use the seatbelt.
- How to locate the doors and other exits.

Flight Attendant
Carrie Bodum

- Rows of emergency lights on the floor that show you the way to the nearest exit.
- Oxygen masks that will drop from the ceiling if the cabin loses air pressure.
- How to fit and use your lifejacket.

Do not ignore this stuff!
Many people do not pay attention to the Safety Demonstration and can't remember anything that was said. Almost certainly you will never need this knowledge—but surely it is better to have paid attention. It is cheap entertainment and great stuff to know!

We can't make you listen, but you are nuts if you don't. Remember, YOU ARE IN CONTROL, of yourself and of how much knowledge you have about *your* aeroplane.

Pay attention during the safety demonstration!

Learn More About Flying

One of the best defences in life is to...

Know Thy Enemy!

If flying is your nemesis learning more about it can really help. You've made a great start by doing this course, but don't stop there!

Lack of knowledge about a topic allows your imagination to run wild and a fear dragon to grow. Educate yourself and this will not happen.

TRY TO FIND INFORMATION THAT...

1. Doesn't treat you like an idiot but also is not too complicated;

2. Is believable and doesn't make you feel like you are being lied to.

Many aviation "news" stories are presented with the motivation of making you afraid. Such lies are *not* helpful! You can do better than relying solely on news services for wisdom.

Here are some suggestions for info:

Bookshops and libraries have loads of books about various aviation topics and are quite good places for a nap.

You can **search the Internet** for topics that interest or concern you. Don't rely on the Internet alone—some of it is bogus—but there is some good stuff too.

- 183 -

Your **airline** has a **website**. There will be information about their aircraft and any special procedures or requirements that they may have. The more you know before you get to the airport the better—unless you like surprises, of course!

The major **aircraft manufacturers** have lots of good stuff on their websites about their aircraft. For example:

Boeing   www.boeing.com
Airbus   www.airbus.com
Embraer   www.embraer.com
Bombardier www.bombardier.com

Airport websites: You might also look at the website for your departure and destination airports. These sites often have quite detailed information, images and maps, giving you a feel for the airport and what to expect when you arrive.

Don't forget the website for this book, **dragonsofthinair.com** for supporting info, and our other site **juniorflyer.com** for a bunch of light hearted and entertaining information on a range of flying topics presented in a simple and fun style.

> ### *Remember: Imagination takes over where knowledge leaves off!*

Choose Your Airline

You have the power of choice. Life is simpler when there are no decisions to be made, but it is your own free will—your ability and willingness to choose—that puts *you* in control.

By exercising self-determination you will:

- Choose an airline which suits your needs and your personality.
- Support an airline you think is doing a good job, and encourage the other airlines to do better.

In modern aviation your money is as powerful a force as lift and drag!

Which Airline Is Best For Me?

There is no simple answer to this because everyone's priorities and needs are different. Some factors to consider:

- **Ticket price**
  Don't forget to include "hidden" charges (taxes, baggage charges, etc.). You get what you pay for and pay for what you get. Some airlines make this clearer than others.
- **Schedule**
  Do they fly where, and when, I want to go?
- **Safety Record**
  Does the airline have a good record? How did they deal with problems that may have occurred in the past?
- **Past experience**
  Recall your own experiences with this and other airlines.
- **Word-of-mouth recommendations**
  What have friends, workmates, travel writers, bloggers, etc., had to say about their experiences with this airline?
- **Convenience**
  Is the whole experience, from check-in through to collecting your bags at the other end, likely to be a (reasonably) painless experience?
- **Humaneness, Respect and Staff Attitude**
  Do they treat me as a valued customer? Am I treated with respect, rather than as "walking cargo?" Happy, pleasant and helpful staff make the whole experience better, and suggest a pride in their airline.
- **Vibe**
  Do I have a good overall feeling about this airline? Do I respect their values and way of doing business?

As you can see, there are many issues to consider.

Is It Important Which Airline I Choose?

From a safety perspective, it probably doesn't make a huge difference. In most countries Government laws and regulations require airlines to behave in a responsible way. The aeroplanes airlines use are basically the same, all being generally considered "safe." It is likely, therefore, that all of those airlines provide a reasonable level of safety.

Having said that, there *are* slight differences in the level of safety provided by each airline. Things like how the crew are trained and the priorities and motivations of the airline's managers come into play. These things can be difficult for an outsider to determine.

> ### *Decide your priorities and ask questions*
> ### *BEFORE buying your ticket.*

TIP: If you are not happy with a particular airline then *buy a ticket with a different airline!* Spend your money wisely and you will make aviation better and safer.

Remember, *you are in control* of your situation right from the start, even before you have bought your ticket!

Most importantly, RELAX!
Take some deep breaths.

YOU

ARE

IN

CONTROL!

Maximum Safety

"Does it matter which airline we choose?" asked Larry. "You have told us that flying is safe. Why should we bother getting tricky about choosing our airline?"

"You are right, Larry. It probably makes no difference at all, and if it doesn't worry you then don't feel that it should."

"Then why suggest that we take an interest in choosing an airline that is right for us?"

"Well," smiled the dragon, "it's all about balls."

The Walkers were unsure how to take this piece of advice, so I explained, reminding them of their visit to the Fear Dragons pool.

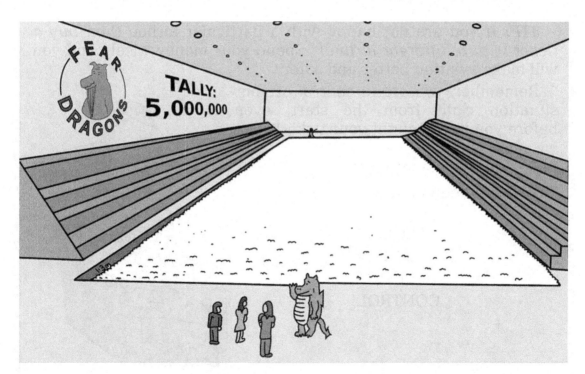

"The average safety statistic, for all airlines across the globe, is an Olympic size pool approximately one metre deep filled with tennis balls. That is an awesome number of balls."

"What about the lower end of the safety scale?"

"That is polite language, Larry. Say what you really mean."

"Okay, Felix. Let's not beat about the bush. How many balls are in the pool for the worst airlines? What are my chances of dying then?"

"That depends, but it can be as low as 40 centimetres, or 8 inches of tennis balls. Bear in mind, that is over the entire size of an Olympic pool so it is still a lot of balls. The chances of picking your ball out of that pool are still amazingly small."

"And what about the best? What if we pay extra money and only fly on the best airlines — airlines with excellent records; airlines that tell the truth, to us and to themselves, and are not afraid to admit their mistakes; airlines that make safety and honesty their number-one priorities. How many balls would there be then?"

"That's a great question, Larry. For the best airlines in the world you could estimate their safety statistics as an Olympic size swimming pool 2 metres deep filled with tennis balls. That's nearly 7 feet deep over the whole pool... you couldn't touch the bottom if you jumped in!"

"Wow!" said Johnny. "That's a lot of balls."

"The more balls the better, if you ask me," said Larry.

I smacked my forehead with my claw. "You have just reminded me. I have some T-shirts for you, as prizes for doing my course. This one is for you, Larry. It will remind you of why you are here."

I tossed the shirt to Larry, and then gave the other Walkers a T-shirt, each with a different slogan or phrase.

Larry put his new T-shirt on over his other clothes and admired its simple printed advice. *More Balls* was an important concept in the aviation world, and Larry knew it.

I told them a sad truth about my job as a Fear Dragon: "The best airlines require more balls than we can fit in our pool to demonstrate their level of safety. That makes my fear job very difficult."

"What do you mean, Felix?" asked Jane.

"Well, to make someone afraid of something so safe, safer than driving in a car, safer even than staying at home, much of the time, takes an awful amount of creativity. I actually have to lie my tail off to get away with it!"

The Walkers, wearing their attractive new T-shirts, were unconcerned. They knew they would not believe my lies any more.

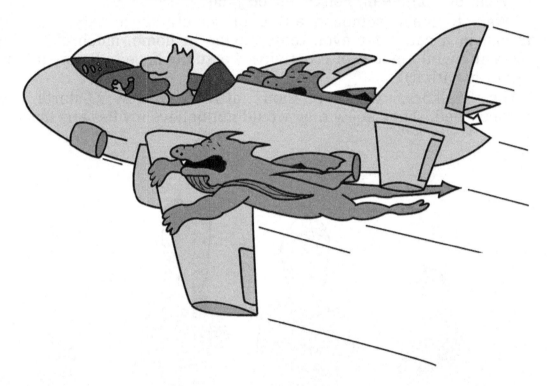

Lesson 14: Where To From Here?

Life is full of choices. Sometimes it may seem that events have made our choices for us and we may not be entirely happy with where we have ended up.

Behind all of this, however, were our own decisions. Was it compulsory to believe that flying is dangerous? Up until now, have you may have avoided learning more about the things that scare you, allowing a fear dragon to affect your life. As a person with free will, this was a choice that *you* made.

We all have choices.

The great thing about free will is that it can be exercised at any time. There is no time when we cannot make a new choice; we cannot rewrite the past, but we *can* choose a better future.

If being a nervous flyer, or a non-flyer, has become a part of your story, you can rewrite that story. That is a matter of choice.

There are some things that, at face value, are not optional. Anxiety and the *run-or-fight* fear response are wired into us by millions of years of evolution. How do you change that?

The *run-or-fight* reflex cannot be eliminated— you will always jump the first time a screeching cat leaps out of the refrigerator—but the triggers for that response *can* be changed. After watching the same horror movie several times you will not jump when the cat leaps out because your brain knows it is coming and knows that it is not dangerous. Even the scariest movie gets boring when you've seen it a few times.

The keys to this "yawn effect" are *belief and familiarity*. If you believe that something is not dangerous or scary then your body's automatic anxiety and fear responses will not be triggered. This belief comes from exposure to the truth and eliminating the misunderstandings and lies from your story.

This course has been designed to give you some exposure to aspects of flying that can be troublesome. Read it, understand it, and then read it again! When the topics are familiar and boring they will be scary no longer.

Fear of Flying courses and psychologists can be beneficial. Aside from providing behind-the-scenes information about flying, many of these courses include real hands-on stuff. They may take you aboard a parked plane for a look around, give you a chance to fly a flight simulator yourself, and take you on an actual flight with your classmates. Nothing beats this kind of real-world exposure for showing you, in a way that you can believe, that flying is safe.

There are other ways too. Some people have faced their fear of flying by learning to fly! That's not as crazy as it sounds; flying schools are friendly places that will work with you. Tell them why you are thinking of taking flying lessons and they will structure a course to suit you, at a speed that you are comfortable with. Don't be daunted—you already know the most important stuff!

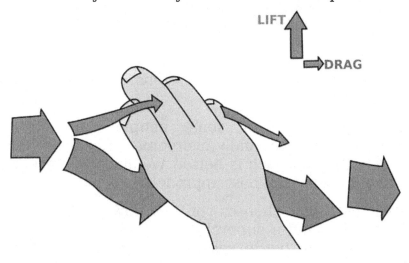

A goal of these lessons has been to show how your mind creates its own scary movie, a fiction based on misunderstandings, half-truths and lies. Fed fertiliser like this, your imagination will create a worst-case vision of doom. I call this talent "the artistry of the mind."

We have used dragons as a symbol of your storytelling gift because they are fictional creatures of terror. Sure, the dragons here are not so scary, but we want to help you become less afraid of flying rather than more afraid of dragons!

Overcoming fear is a process of steps, each step requiring a decision and a little courage.

Gradual steps work for some people, building on each preceding success to eventually overcome large fears. For others, the "leap of faith" approach is better. We are all different and you will have to determine the best approach for you.

Whichever path you choose, you are now armed with a great deal of knowledge and a supercharged mind that will not accept lies. Your stories will better resemble the truth and therefore be less frightening.

Each flight from now on will get easier, just as a scary movie becomes *not*-scary after you have seen it a few times.

Be aware of your own emotional state and level of tension, so that you can take steps to prevent a "tension tornado." If you feel yourself being drawn down this path remember that *relaxation techniques* can break the cycle of tension, anxiety and fear.

Stop, breathe, let-go, think safe.

Your imagination, while being a wonderful thing, can lead you on an unpleasant journey. If the "facts" you have about a topic are wrong or incomplete then your imagination will create an explanation which is wrong. Your mind is a fabulous storyteller... *be aware of the fictions it can create!*

You are in control. By making this choice you will realise that fear no longer limits you and you will realise your dreams. As your experience grows you will see that your fears were nothing more than *dragons of thin air.*

**Thanks for completing these lessons,
and best wishes for your quest
to slay <u>your</u> personal fear dragon!**

Oh, one more thing. Has anyone seen my phone?

Course Wrap-Up

"Well, that's about it. We seem to have come to the end of the slides, and I don't have much more to tell you about fear of flying. It must be time for your test."

"What?" exclaimed Larry. "You never said anything about a test!" Larry could feel the knot forming in his belly already.

"Relax, my friends. You will not find it difficult if you have been paying attention. Here it is: I want you to talk about what you have learned today, then write one sentence on the whiteboard that summarises *everything*."

Larry was relieved, but Louise protested, "We have learned so much! How can we wrap it all into one sentence?"

"Just do your best. One sentence only! You will then use this sentence any time you feel tense or anxious about flying, to remind yourself about all that you have learned."

So the family gathered together and discussed the day's events, knowing that this would not be easy.

Johnny had liked the tennis balls; Jane had liked learning about the tension tornado. Larry had *not* liked it when I almost bit his head off, but he had learned a valuable lesson about his body's automatic responses to fear. Louise now knew how awareness of fear pulling your strings gives you a chance to cut those strings.

So much knowledge, but how to summarise it all?

Larry had an idea and discussed it with the others. They agreed, so he wrote it on the board.

Larry's words, "Flying is Safe and Fun," were the very words with which I had commenced the course. At the time, the Walkers had considered this too short, but now it did seem to be a good summary.

I clapped my paws. "Well done, my new friends. You have indeed got it!"

The Walkers did seem pleased with themselves.

"Apparently, good instructors ask their students for feedback about the course, to help them make their presentation better for next time. While it is unlikely that I could present this course in a more perfect manner, do you have any suggestions or comments?"

Larry raised his hand. "There's just one thing Felix. I gather that many fear of flying courses end up by taking the students on an actual flight. This course has been good, but perhaps a little theoretical."

"Of course! I almost forgot! I have to give you your air tickets!"

The family seemed surprised, but they really had earned a reward. What better than a flight?

I handed them four very special boarding passes. Sometimes simply holding a boarding pass is enough to trigger a fearful flyer's anxiety, but this did not happen to the Walkers.

They looked at their tickets, wondering where and when they would be going flying.

Louise asked, "Er, Felix? These tickets don't show the airline. They are just labelled 'Fear Dragons.' Do you guys have your own planes?"

"No, of course not, and I did mention to you earlier that my budget is quite low. I do want you to go flying, however, to solidify your new understanding."

I walked over to the door and called out into the hallway, to the three dragons waiting outside. "Come in, come in!"

To the Walkers I said, "I'd like to introduce you to some friends who are going to help us out today. This is Foxy Fear, Flat Earth Garcia and Doctor Leroy Amygdala."

With some hesitation, my three friends entered the room. They were obviously nervous about being there, but then the idea of helping humans rather than frightening them was very new. Foxy, ravishing as always, gave me a wink. Old Garcia walked slowly, his too-long toenails giving him some grief; Doc Leroy nearly tripped over, his sunglasses being far too dark for the dimly lit storeroom.

My old mentor, Flat Earth Garcia, gave a dry, toothless grin to the kids and then addressed the class:

"Welcome, family Walker. Thankyou for coming today. I hope it has been... uplifting. We are all very proud of Felix, and what he has done to put this course together. It is a new thing for us to help people overcome fear, rather than cause it. We are watching his experiment with interest."

The Walkers chatted with my dragon friends for a while, discussing some of the interesting things they had learned and asking about the Fear Dragons. Eventually, their conversation returned to their boarding passes.

"I don't understand," said Larry. "Each of these air tickets says 'SEAT 1A'. How can that be?"

"Quite simple, my friends. Because each is front row, the best seat on board! You will all be travelling First Class."

I led the group, humans and dragons together, up to the roof of Fear Dragon Headquarters. Each dragon paired up with one of the students, and the nature of the flight they were about to undertake became clear.

I was proud of my students. They had learned so much, progressed so far. "Well done today! Facing your fears takes courage, and you have done well. Now you are going to get the flight of your lives. If you can fly with the Fear Dragons, flying on an airliner will be child's play for you. Are you up for it?"

"Yes," said Johnny, who was never afraid in the first place. "I want to fly!"

Larry, Louise and Jane nodded. They were confident that they could meet the challenges of flight with an open mind and an open heart. They knew that they could now fly without fear.

So, each of my new human friends, perched on the back of a dragon between powerful wings, launched into the sky.

Humans and dragons, together, flew merrily and laughed aloud, frolicking amongst the clouds in the warm light of the afternoon sun.

And the Walkers flew happily ever after.

Felix
Fear Dragon - Aviation Specialist
Winner: 3 times World Aviation Fear Champion

Presenter: A Most Unusual Fear of Flying Course

Appendix:
Dragon Slayers

This book is written to help you hunt your own dragon, but you may want some help in your noble quest. There are plenty of experienced psychologists and excellent courses available to help. These people are professional dragon slayers!

We list these courses and resources on our website. Feel free to visit us at:

dragonsofthinair.com

You will find links and contact details for:

- Airline sponsored *Fear of Flying* Courses
- Independent *Fear of Flying* Courses
- *Fear of Flying* information websites
- Blogs and Forums about *Fear of Flying*
- *Fear of Flying* Book and DVD reviews
- Fear of Flying books to buy

You might also like to send us your thoughts and comments about this book. We'd love to hear from you.   You can contact us via our website:

dragonsofthinair.com

Sleigh Your Fear Dragon!

Index

CPSIA information can be obtained
at www.ICGtesting.com
Printed in the USA
LVOW03s1021181215

467147LV00012B/418/P

9 781450 549561